PROVISIONS

FOR THE

Journey

*A 31 Day Roadmap to Breakthroughs
through Fasting, Prayer, and Planning*

MARK A. MOORE, SR.

Limits of Liability and Disclaimer of Warranty

The author and publisher shall not be liable for your misuse of this material. This book is strictly for informational and educational purposes. The purpose of this book is to educate and entertain. The author and/or publisher do not guarantee that anyone following these techniques, suggestions, tips, ideas, or strategies will become successful. The author and/or publisher shall have neither liability nor responsibility to anyone with respect to any loss or damage caused, or alleged to be caused, directly or indirectly by the information contained in this book.

Unless otherwise indicated, Bible quotations in are from the Holy Bible, New International Version®, NIV. Copyright © 1973, 1978, 1984 by International Bible Society. Used by permission of Zondervan. All Rights Reserved.

Other Bible quotations are from The New Revised Standard Version of the Bible © 1989 by the Division of Christian Education of the National Council of the Churches of Christ in the U.S.A. Used by permission. All rights reserved.

The King James Version ® Copyright © 1982 by Thomas Nelson, Inc. Used by permission. All rights reserved.

Views expressed in this publication do not necessarily reflect the views of the publisher.

Cover Design: J. Designs (www.jdesignsonline.com)

Printed in the United States of America

ISBN 978-0-9990740-4-6

Keen Vision Publishing, LLC

www.keen-vision.com

*For my parents, the late Bishop Benjamin T. Moore &
Dr. Willa Moore, who taught me to love God and serve
His people*

ACKNOWLEDGEMENTS

To my wife, Shirley, and our three wonderful children – Mark, Jr., George and Sharon – who have been a constant source of love, laughter and encouragement.

To my college classmate, turned editor, Rev. Chantaye Elmore Knotts – you have the distinction of being one of my oldest friends, and thankfully, you have never allowed me to forget it!

To the Faith Covenant Church of Jesus Christ Family (Atlanta, GA) – thanks for allowing me to practice pastoring on you for the past 20 years!

To the members of Zion Temple Church (Havre De Grace, MD), my first pastorate – thanks for accepting a young pastor & his family and loving us unconditionally!

To my Pastor, Bishop James D. Nelson, Sr. – when my father passed, I thought there could never be another father-figure in my life. You proved me wrong! May you and Mother Nelson live forever!

WHAT PASTORS & LEADERS ARE SAYING...

"As I began reading this devotional, I thought of the classic by A.W. Tozer written in 1959 entitled, Born After Midnight. This book has the same quality and impact. The words carefully used, the strategically placed quotes from other writers, and the relevant application of ancient truths all lead me to believe that this is an instant classic read for the post-modern church. Though a trained theologian, Bishop Mark Moore has not presented a sterile antiseptic book filled with theories and philosophical jargon - no, you'll find that he acknowledges his own struggles with this very challenging subject which gives the readers hope. If you use this devotional while fasting, you will find a "fullness" filling your belly that did not come from food - but from the words of this devotional."

Bishop Joel D. Trout
Harvest Time Apostolic
Ministries Riverdale, GA

"The sentiments and passions of a hungry worshipper have been captured by the pen of Bishop Moore. Only a true worshipper could write a devotional like this one. Clearly, the author wants more of God. I think his readers will too. This book is sure to be a classic!"

Bishop John Fonzer
Pastor/Author
Moss Point, MS

"In my humble opinion this devotional book is certainly a major tool strategically designed to usher believers into an intimate and authentic RELATIONSHIP with God! Not only do I endorse the authored words, I also firmly endorse the vessel God has used to author these words, Bishop Mark A. Moore, Sr."

Bishop Samuel Blakes
New Home Family Worship Center
New Orleans & Baton Rouge, LA

"Bishop Mark Moore, Sr., is the consummate teacher and spiritual father to an entire generation of leaders. No doubt this book is sure to bring clarity and helpful instruction to those seeking to strengthen their understanding of prayer and fasting. With keen insight, wisdom, and practicality, this book is sure to become a "go to" source for both the inexperienced and the seasoned saint!"

Pastor Timothy Findley, Jr.
Pastor / Founder – Kingdom Life Fellowship
Louisville, KY

"Spiritually stimulating!! Enriching!! Consecration is not event, but a continuing, life transforming experience. Bishop Mark Moore has given us the prescription God sent. Let's TAKE THE JOURNEY!!! Proud of you SON!!!"

Bishop James D. Nelson, Sr.,
Founder – World Assemblies of Restoration
Baltimore, MD

"Provisions for the journey is as a spiritual navigation system leading to deeper intimacy with God and personal productivity. It is replete with scriptural signposts and turn-by-turn directions. Bishop Moore has supplied the Body of Christ with a jewel. It promotes the spiritual disciplines of journaling and prayer and is a call to personal initiative. This work is a must for individuals and entire congregations."

Bishop R.C. Blakes, Jr.
Presiding Bishop, Family of Churches Fellowship International
New Orleans, LA and Houston, TX

"Bishop Mark Moore is definitely one of the exciting ministers of this time! His passion comes right in your face as he presents the Word of God. Enjoy the sincere and insightful conversation you will gain from his writings."

Bishop James G. Rodges
Pastor, Jonesville Baptist Church of the P.A.W.
Savannah, GA

CONTENTS

Introduction
You Can Get There From Here

Every successful journey requires three things: A starting point, an ending point, and a reason. Sometimes the starting point or the ending point IS the reason. Journeys are often motivated by a burning desire to be away from something or an equally strong desire to get to something.

The fact that you are holding this book tells me one thing about you: You are contemplating a "Journey." I don't know your starting point or your reason, but I know you are considering making a move. You may already be packed and fueled up.

Allow me then to talk a bit about the destination. It is a place many talk about, few seek, and even fewer find. Yet, it is accessible to all who sincerely search for it. Every saint who has been greatly used of God to make an impact in this world was transformed and equipped there. It is the place where Divine Direction becomes distinguishable, and assignments become apparent. The psalmist called it a "secret place" (Psalm 91:1), not because it is hidden from those who seek it with a pure heart, but because it is a place of safety and security. In fact, you and I are invited to go there. Will you accept the invitation?

It is the destination of a lifetime - the place your heart has longed for and the place your soul has craved even when you couldn't find the words to articulate your yearning. It is the place of joy, peace, purpose, privilege, and power. It is the place of consistent victory and unembarrassed intimacy with the Father. More than that, it is also the place of realized potentials and fulfilled personal dreams. It is the place of life lived to the fullest. Do you want to go?

"If it is all that," some might ask, "then why aren't more people there, or at least on their way?" Perhaps it is because of the whole "unembarrassed intimacy with the Father" thing. Most of us suffer from "intimacy" issues, particularly as it relates to the Almighty. Isn't it ironic that we seek to hide from the One from Whom it is absolutely impossible to remain concealed? We come by this tendency honestly, I suppose. Our grandparents, Adam and Eve, attempted to hide from Him in the Garden. Most of their descendants throughout history have tended to be somewhat cagey regarding "full disclosure" with God. Many miss out on the journey of a lifetime, simply because they instinctively know that the cost of admission to that "place" in God is their "fig leaves."

To embark upon this "Journey" is to answer the call to higher ground. Another reason most people don't attempt the Journey is that ascending requires effort. It requires leaving the comfort zone of the lowlands. Going higher means elevating one's vision, values, standards, and exertion. We have settled for mediocrity for so long that many of us have come to feel superior because we are the one-eyed elite in the Valley of the Blind. For most so-called Christians, the entire extent of their relationship with God amounts to nothing more than church membership – no growth, progression, maturation in Christ, or ascent to "higher ground." Salvation is "fire insurance" just in case there is a hell. In the meantime, so much of life here on earth seems to be anything but what they signed up for.

You're still reading. I'm feeling more and more confident that you're ready for something different. You are ready for something better than you've ever experienced before. You're ready for the "Journey!" So let's be clear, you are about to move into a closer relationship with God than you may have ever thought possible. More than that, you are about to learn first-hand just what Jesus meant when He said, "...I am come that they might have life, and that they might have it more abundantly." (John 10: 10). Your life – every aspect of it – is about to take a turn for the better! The "end point" of this "Journey" is a life lived in the presence of God, resulting in incredible peace, purpose, power, and prosperity.

Every successful journey requires a starting point, an ending point, and a reason. But there is more. Every successful journey requires a route. This "Journey" is no exception. The route for this "Journey" is notoriously narrow but has proven reliable over centuries of use. It has been traveled by the famous, and by those called nobodies. Over the centuries, it has delivered every earnest traveler safely to his destination. It is the "route" of fasting, prayer, and planning.

Here is where things get tricky. Most of us KNOW far more about fasting, prayer, and planning than we have ever put into practice. Familiarity can be the enemy of fulfillment. John H. Jowett, a pulpit giant of the early 20th Century, once warned of the danger of a "deadening familiarity with the sublime." He cautioned that it is possible to become "professors but not pilgrims," and to "indicate the way, but not be found in it" (Jowett, The Preacher: His Life and Work).

To bring it into more modern parlance – the fact that you have watched the Travel Channel on television doesn't actually mean you're a "world traveler." Fasting, prayer, and planning are such familiar concepts that we tend to automatically think we are experts. Here's the painful reality: Most people we know put more effort into planning vacations than planning their lives. Most people sing more about prayer in church than they ever actually pray at home. For most people, "fasting" is a foreign term that roughly translates to "pre-surgical dietary deprivation."

Most of us at least understand the importance of planning and the importance of prayer. But why fast? How will fasting along with prayer and planning produce different results than we have seen in the past? In a word, fasting is a spiritual "octane booster" that turbo-charges prayer and planning. It is the gateway to natural and supernatural breakthrough.

What is fasting? Fasting is abstinence from nourishment (food and/or drink) and pleasure for the purpose of devoting oneself to the Lord. In the Old Testament fasting was sometimes referred to as "afflicting the soul" (Leviticus 23: 27, 29; Isaiah 58: 5), and as "humbling oneself" (Psalm 35: 13; Psalm 69: 10; Ezra 8: 21). It is a purposeful act of discipline born of a desire to dedicate oneself to the Lord.

In Isaiah 58:5, the prophet describes fasting as a "day for a man to afflict his soul." In Psalm 69:10, David says he "chastened" his soul with fasting. In Psalm 35:13, he says he "humbled" his soul by abstaining from food. Let us bear in mind that humility is not a vague emotion, but rather it is something very specific.

Humility is an attitude of the heart. The Scripture says, "A broken and contrite heart – these, O God, You will not despise." (Psalm 51:17). God hears us and responds to our cries when we come before Him in humility and brokenness. Further, when we humble ourselves before God, He, in turn, exalts us (Matthew 23: 12). The choice is ours. Do we want to be abased or do we want to be exalted? If we exalt ourselves, we shall be humbled by the Almighty; but if we humble ourselves, He has promised to exalt us.

Fasting, when combined with prayer produces amazing results! Together, fasting with prayer can result in a spiritual atomic bomb that pulls down spiritual strongholds and releases the power of God in your life and the lives of the individuals in your family and your church. I love what Dr. Tony Evans once said: "When we fast, we are saying that the cry of our souls is greater than the cry of our stomachs."

Down through the ages, those who have done mighty things for God have testified to the necessity of prayer with fasting. According to reliable church tradition and recorded history, for centuries, most of the church world practiced fasting regularly on Wednesday and Friday of every week. These were the two days normally recognized for fasting.

The early Methodists under John and Charles Wesley regularly practiced fasting. It was a normal part of their lifestyle, although few of today's Methodists follow the same routine. John Wesley so believed in the power of fasting and prayer, that he not only urged the early Methodists to fast and pray every Wednesday and Friday, but he refused to ordain anyone in Methodism who wouldn't agree to fast. The roll call of other great Christian leaders who determined to make prayer with fasting a part of their lives reads like a hall of fame: Martin Luther, John Calvin, John Knox, Jonathan Edwards, Matthew Henry,

Charles Finney, Andrew Murray, D. Martyn Lloyd- Jones, and many more.

Why should we fast today? In addition to humbling ourselves, other powerful motives for fasting, include:

- ➤ To draw closer to God – "draw near to God...He will draw near to you" – James 4: 8.
- ➤ To find God's will and to receive His direction for our lives – Ezra said, "I proclaimed a fast there, at the river of Ahava, that we might afflict ourselves before our God to seek a right way for our little ones and for all our substance." (Ezra 8: 21)
- ➤ To seek divine healing and deliverance - "Thine health shall spring forth speedily." (Isaiah 58: 8) Jesus also taught about certain kinds of evil spirits that "This kind goeth not out but by prayer and fasting." (Matthew 17: 21)
- ➤ To seek for divine intervention in a time of crisis – In 2 Chronicles 20, one of the kings of ancient Judah, Jehoshaphat, along with his nation found themselves being invaded by a superior army. Instead of resorting to human ingenuity, they humbled themselves, fasted, and prayed. God dealt so decisively with the invading army that the people of Judah didn't have to use a single weapon. God totally defeated their enemies.
- ➤ To intercede and pray on behalf of others – fasting demonstrates a level of love and faith that is willing to make personal sacrifices for someone else's benefit!

Should we fast in this day and time? We should fast only if we feel the need to humble ourselves before God, draw closer to Him, or seek His guidance, healing, or direction. Should we fast? We should fast if we feel the burden to successfully intercede for others in our lives or feel a cry in our souls that is greater than the cry of our stomachs!

In the writings of the prophet Isaiah (Isaiah 58: 8-12), we find at least ten specific promises for those who fast according to the will of God:

> ➢ Light
> ➢ Health
> ➢ Righteousness
> ➢ Glory
> ➢ Answered prayer
> ➢ Continual guidance
> ➢ Satisfaction
> ➢ Refreshing
> ➢ Work that endures
> ➢ Restoration

What Christian in their right mind would not desire to take advantage of such benefits?

Still, fasting seems to have fallen on hard times. Perhaps it is because Bible reading has all but been abandoned. Fasting has been dumbed down to the point of irrelevance. It is not uncommon nowadays to hear people talk about "fasting" from nighttime until the next morning – most of which time they are asleep anyway. Or, people are urged to fast an hour or to skip a solitary meal – as if these things don't happen in the normal ebb and flow of weekly life. Fasting, real fasting, is uncomfortable. So, authentic fasting – the kind that afflicts the soul – is taboo. Yet we wonder why personal and corporate breakthroughs are so elusive and rare.

What then, does biblical fasting look like? There are three primary kinds of fasts described in the Scriptures:

➤ The Normal Fast – no food of any kind is to be eaten, but only water is consumed (unsweetened juices, and clear broth if needed for strength). This is the kind of fast that Jesus embarked upon at the beginning of His ministry (40 days in the Wilderness, Matthew 4: 2). This kind of fasting can be powerful for clarifying one's assignment and identity.

➤ The Absolute Fast – no food or drinks of any kind are taken for a set amount of time. For example, from the time one goes to bed until dinner the following day, or for two or three days. This fast was recorded in Esther 4:16 when the exiled Jews were in danger of genocide. It was a fast of urgency that brought about supernatural deliverance.

➤ The Daniel Fast – fruit, vegetables, juices, and water only – no meat, sweets, or bread. This fast was engaged by the Prophet Daniel for some 21 days as he sought for wisdom and guidance - Daniel 10: 3; 1: 8-14.

If you're a part of that powerful minority for whom the cry of your soul is greater than the cry of your stomach....if you have decided that the pain of staying as you have been is greater than the pain of moving out of the rut of your "comfort zone"... if you have determined that this year is going to be your year to search out the promise of Abundant Life – spiritually, naturally, relationally and yes, even financially – then this book is for you!

Provisions for the Journey is not just another devotional. If you're looking for a daily dose of three paragraphs, a poem, and a prayer, this book isn't for you. However, if you're looking for a book that will challenge you to think, evaluate, pray, and plan, you're holding the right book! Provisions for the Journey is intended to be a roadmap and inspirational companion for those who are on the "road" to breakthroughs in every area of their lives and are willing to take the arduous route of fasting, prayer, and planning. I know from over 40 years of experience that fasting and prayer can be a lonely business. So, this book is purposed to be an encouraging daily voice, a voice that challenges and cheers you toward your potential.

This is a compendium of 31 transformational devotional writings complete with suggestions for the disciplines of journaling, prayer, and Scripture reading. There's more. After every seven days, you will encounter a "Fuel Stop," a practical challenge aimed at helping you map out the life of your dreams through vision clarification, goal setting, action plans, and affirmations.

Are you ready for your change? If so, then no matter where you are right now, or what your reason is for taking on the challenge of climbing to higher ground, just get on the "route," and you can get there!

Day One
How Much of God Do You Want?

Focus Verse: *"Blessed are those who hunger and thirst for righteousness, for they will be filled."* (Matthew 5: 6)

There were probably no angels at your bedside this morning as you awoke. I imagine there was no heavenly harp music to call you from your bed into the place of prayer - only the solemn realization that you opened your big mouth and made a commitment to consecrate and seek the Lord. At moments like this, we must remind ourselves that much of our walk with God has nothing to do with our feelings. We stand on the promises of God, not our emotions. So, whether we feel like it or not, we begin this journey toward God's purposes and promises for our life. Pastor Jentezen Franklin, a leading proponent of fasting, once said:

> "Fasting brings one into a deeper, more intimate, and powerful relationship with the LORD. When you eliminate food from your diet for a number of days, your spirit becomes uncluttered by the things of this world and

amazingly sensitive to the things of God."

King David said:

> "As the deer pants for the water brooks so my soul pants for you, O God. My soul thirsts for God, for the living God. When shall I come and appear before God? My tears have been my food day and night, while they continually say to me, "Where is your God?" (Psalm 42: 1-3 NKJV)

At times like this, I find myself drawn to the words of a poem by a preacher/writer named Wilbur Rees, "3 Dollars' Worth of God." It is one of my favorite poems because it expresses my struggle with the Christian life.

3 Dollars' Worth of God

I would like to buy 3 dollars' worth of God, please.
Not enough to explode my soul or disturb my sleep,
But just enough to equal a cup of warm milk, or a snooze in the sunshine.
I don't want enough of Him to make me love a black man, or pick beets with a migrant.
I want ecstasy not transformation.
I want the warmth of the womb, not a new birth.
I want a pound of the eternal in a paper sack.
I would like to buy 3 dollars' worth of God, please.

This poem touches me, not just because it voices the unspoken sentiments and values of so many people I encounter in day-to-day ministry, but also because it gives voice to the unspoken sentiments I struggle to overcome in my own life. How much of God do I really want?

The "spirit of the age" infects all of us, at some level, with the temptation to view our relationship with God as an optional convenience – something to be managed and fit into our busy lives as we see fit. We tend to "cut" God into doable doses. We ration His influence in our lives into scripted, stained-glass moments that won't interfere with our plans or cramp our style. Many of us, present company included, manage God with the precision of a pharmacist. Too much of Him might (in the words of the poem) "...explode my soul or disturb my sleep;" While too little of Him leaves me with a gnawing emptiness, sin sickness, and a grinding guilt headache. The "proper" dosage results in warmth, comfort, and ecstasy. "Overdosing" results in radical transformation and cataclysmic re-birth...and we all know how messy that can get.

I, too, struggle with answering the question: How much of God do I really want? There are times in my life when I want a "pound of the eternal in a paper sack." In the words of Bill Hybels, "Who doesn't prefer ecstasy and euphoria to commitment and personal sacrifice?" I struggle with how much of God I want in my life, or more accurately, how much of my life I want Him to control. Admittedly, I am inclined to seek just enough of Him to feel warm and fuzzy, or maybe on a rare occasion, just enough to feel righteously indignant about the injustice in the world. But enough to get up off my seat and live a changed life? Well, that's another question.

I suspect, if we are honest, we must admit that all of us struggle, at least a little bit, with managing our level of commitment to God. The popular term for it in this day and age is "balance." Balance is a useful word when speaking of things about which we are not passionate. People in love know that passion knows no such thing as "balance." Greatness knows no balance, either. Greatness comes only to those who attempt far more than the "balanced" masses deem fitting or proper. Greatness always exceeds the boundaries of "balance."

For most of us, the struggle centers more on our desire for comfort and unconditional acceptance than anything else. We want a God who won't demand too much – a reasonable, domesticated Deity. And, we prefer a "Reader's Digest" Bible, devoid of any offensive content. We seem to admire and flock after those leaders who have been most successful in their quest to remake the Church of Jesus Christ into an international "chain store" where the "customer is always right" – even when they happen to be wrong.

A well-intentioned follower lamented not long ago that some of his guests felt a bit uncomfortable at our church because our adherence to the message and methods of the New Testament Church caused them to question their salvation. As gently as I could, I tried to express that the ministry of the Church is not about making people feel comfortable as they are. The message of Jesus Christ is divisive and uncomfortable to most religious people. Still, most modern Christians require fashionable, feel-good churches that don't overly challenge them or exercise too much "control." The Church of today isn't much for confronting or commanding repentance or conversion – it is much bigger on soothing and suggesting. We want "the warmth of the womb, not a new birth."

The poem reminds me of our collective struggle as people of faith who must choose between the culture of the modern so-called Church and the authentic Christianity of the Bible. It reminds me of our struggle as people who must decide between a "pound of the eternal" or the God of eternity. Here's the awesome truth: Even though having a manageable, domesticated Deity is tempting, that's not really what our deepest self, the core of our existence, calls for.

So, on this first day of our spiritual makeover, we must settle these troubling questions: How much of God do we really want? And, which God do we want - the stained-glass, rose-tinted God who promises never to rain on our parade, or the dangerous, unpredictable, and yet loving Almighty God of the Bible, who makes all of life an adventure?

The New Testament book of James offers the following key to victory in the Christian walk:

"Submit yourselves therefore to God. Resist the devil, and he will flee from you. Draw nigh to God and He will draw nigh to you..." James 4: 7, 8a (NKJV)

TAKE ACTION!

Thoughts for your Journal:

> ➢ How "much" of God do you really want?
> ➢ How "much" of yourself are you willing to give God this year?
> ➢ In what areas have you previously or habitually withheld full obedience to God?

Prayer Focus:
During this Journey (drawing closer to God), pray that God will instill in you a greater desire for authentic relationship with Him!

Suggested Bible Reading:

> ➢ Psalm 42
> ➢ Matthew 5
> ➢ James 4: 6-10

Day Two
Presents or Presence?

Focus Verses: *"Now therefore, I pray thee, if I have found favor in Thy sight, shew me now Thy way, that I may know Thee, that I may find grace in Thy sight and consider that this nation is Thy people...if Thy presence go not with me, carry us not up hence."* (Exodus 33:13, 15 KJV)

Standing on the brink of the fruition of all God had promised to do in his life, Moses turned to the Almighty, "gift receipt" in hand, and essentially said, "Thanks, but no, thanks. If Your Presence doesn't go with us to the Promised Land, I would rather not go." Certainly, this is not a statement that would have been uttered by the masses – not in Moses' day, and surely not in ours. Who among us would willingly forfeit the tangible promises of God's blessings over the intangible, inexplicable "Presence of God"? Anyway, most of us aren't really too sure what the presence of God is. As humans, we often get rituals confused with relationship, and presents confused with presence. We find comfort in going through the motions as long as, in the end, we have something to show for our efforts. We live in a materialistic world. Isn't it only reasonable to choose the visible over the invisible? Why live with nothing to show for it, when you can "get what you get when you go for it"?

Given a choice, Israel chose God's presents over His presence, every time. To be painfully honest, I have chosen presents over the presence more times than I care to admit. I have opted to eat when God called me to fast. I have decided to relax when God called me to pray. I have chosen to watch television when God invited me to spend time in His Word. I have placed my dreams – even those that He implanted within me – above His greater vision for my life, a life lived in partnership as Father and son. Again and again, I have struggled to accomplish something for God – to have something to show for my time on this earth – not realizing that He has never been as concerned with what I can accomplish, as much as He is concerned about what He and I can do together.

The God of Glory doesn't need me to fulfill His will on earth. He can do that by Himself. God delights, however, in the fellowship of the two of us working together to do what He could have done alone. I have missed that fact for years because I was more caught up in the visible present (circumstances), and in the tangible presents (promises and blessings) than I was with the invisible presence. What good is prosperity if it leads me away from God? Of what value is the Promised Land, if God is not there? Without God, it will be no different from any other place. Of what benefit is it to build a great cathedral or to gain the world, but lose the one relationship that truly matters most?

Father, thank You for the many great things you have promised for my future. Thank You for promises of prosperity, favor, and success. I am excited about where you have promised to take me. Forgive me for the times I have forgotten what life is really about; that it is not about the presents, but all about Your Presence. As much as I desire to see Your good promises come to pass in my life, LORD, I resolve here and now that if going into my "Promised Land" means losing the reality of Your Presence, I don't want to go! Help me to live out that commitment in every decision, every day. Thank You! In Jesus' Name, Amen.

TAKE ACTION!

Thoughts for your Journal:
- ➤ What are the "presents" in your life you have chosen over the Presence of God?
- ➤ In light of today's Manna, what changes are in order?

Prayer Focus:
- ➤ Pray that God will help you to surrender every area of your life over to His Lordship.
- ➤ Pray that God will overhaul your priorities – that His Will be done in every area of your life!

Suggested Bible Reading:
- ➤ Exodus 33
- ➤ Psalm 16
- ➤ Psalm 106: 15

Day Three
Get Serious with God!

Focus Verse: *"'Why have we fasted,' they say, 'and you have not sent it? Why have we humbled ourselves and You have not noticed?' Yet on the day of your fasting, you do as you please."* (Isaiah 58:3 NIV)

Most of us are familiar with the words, "Are you serious?" Usually, the implication is that the one being questioned can't possibly be earnest, sincere, or serious. Truth to tell, we're familiar with those words because, at some point, I suspect we have not only asked that question, but have also had to answer it. Something that we said or did stretched the bounds of believability to the breaking point. Or, perhaps, we were known for playing or joking so much that the person asking the question needed to know how to take what we said or did. This is an important question precisely because it identifies the intent of the one being questioned, and it determines the response of the one asking. In other words, if a person is serious about what they said or did, our response will be different than if they are just being frivolous. And so, it is with our pursuit of God.

Here is the make-or-break question that each of us must ask ourselves to determine whether we are on a journey with God or just marching in place: "Am I serious?" Our response will make all the difference in the world. In our focus verse, we see ancient Israel, a frustrated people, addressing an equally frustrated God. To put it in modern terms, they want to know, "What's up with all this fasting and praying when You aren't responding as expected?" God doesn't mince words in His reply: "It's because you aren't really serious about what you're doing!"

Is it possible to go through the motions of religious practices for so long that we delude ourselves into thinking that we have fooled the Almighty? I think it is. In Psalm 50 the Lord has this to say about people who engage in religious behavior without inward integrity: "These things you have done and I kept silent; you thought that I was altogether like you. But I will rebuke you and accuse you to your face." (Psalm 50: 21 NIV). What a rude awakening - to think because judgment hasn't come, it isn't coming, only to find too late that you were sadly mistaken!

As long as Christianity is all about what we want and think we need, and we cloak it under the pretense of being wise or balanced, we're not serious about God! As long as we are ambivalent about what offends God, we're not serious! As long as we're selfish, arrogant or rebellious, WE'RE NOT SERIOUS! As long as we lack in surrender, humility, consistent prayerfulness, repentance, unity or forgiveness, we're not serious! As long as we are placing any other priority above God's plan for our lives, we're not serious! As long as we engage in blame games as to why we're not doing what we should be doing for God, we're not serious! Even if we have deceived everyone else, God knows it!

So, the question for consideration today is simply, "Are you serious?" Are you serious about pursuing purpose? Are you serious about pursuing power in God? Are you serious about being vessels that He can trust as stewards of His prosperity? Or, is it really just all about going through spiritual games and exercises to manipulate God?

I hear Jesus saying, "The Father is seeking true [serious] worshippers to worship Him in Spirit and in Truth" (John 4:23).

TAKE ACTION!

Thoughts for your Journal:
- ➢ What is the last thing God told you to do that you have not yet done? Why?
- ➢ Which personal priorities have placed above His plan for your life? How did you justify it?
- ➢ Which things do you still struggle with giving up even though you know they offend God? Why?

Prayer Focus:
Ask the Lord to show you EVERY area in your walk with Him where you haven't been serious. Ask that He help you to amend your ways today!

Suggested Bible Reading:
- ➢ Psalm 50
- ➢ James 4
- ➢ Revelation 3: 14 – 22

Day Four

Spiritual Detox!

Focus Verses: *"Who can understand his errors? Cleanse Thou me from secret faults. Keep back Thy servant also from presumptuous sins; let them not have dominion over me: then shall I be upright, and I shall be innocent from the great transgression."* (Psalm 19:12,13 KJV)

My family and close friends all know that I am prone to attacks of gout - a painful inflammation of certain joints due to a build-up of uric acid in my system. Gout is typically caused by eating too much of certain proteins such as red meats and shell- fish. When the members of my church see me limping about, they know that their Pastor has probably been eating things that are good *to* him but not good *for* him! Strangely, one of the worst attacks of gout that I've ever experienced came when I wasn't eating at all. We were on a 21-day fast and I only had liquids. The onset of gout came sometime after the 7th day of fasting. It started in one foot and moved to the other foot. Within a few days, I was so severely crippled that my wife insisted on taking me to the podiatrist to be checked. In my entire life, I have never been so happy to receive a needle in both feet!

The mystery to me was what had brought on such a severe attack of gout when I wasn't even eating at all. The doctor smiled and explained that the fasting was the reason. Fasting was causing my body to detoxify itself. It was causing impurities and toxins, such as the high levels of uric acid in my joints, to come to the surface so that my system could deal with them and expel them.

What a revelation! The great benefit, and sometimes the great difficulty, of fasting is the detoxification that it sets off in our bodies. Other than hunger, the primary reason most of us find fasting unpleasant has to do with the discomfort that comes from the detox process. The headaches, nausea, bad breath and strange body odors are all symptoms of our bodies' fight to expel toxins that have accumulated unchecked in our systems over time. Literally, we feel bad because we're getting better. If we would press ourselves to fast for more than 4 days (liquids only), most of us would discover that we would begin to feel better than we have for years! Some would even find themselves "miraculously" healed of chronic physical maladies and other problems we never realized were being caused by the toxins hiding in our system!

Just as the pain of physical detoxification works to make us better, so it is in the spiritual. When they fast, most people expect to find themselves on an immediate spiritual high, seeing immediate positive results in their lives, relationships, and even in their church or community. Over many years of fasting, I have discovered that this is not usually the case! Just as fasting brings toxins to the surface in our physical body, it often does the same in the spiritual realm. When we become earnest in fasting and prayer, ugly, toxic things may surface in our lives and in our churches; things that we must confront and expel to go to the next level in spiritual health.

In our focus verse, the psalmist asks, "Who can understand his errors?" If you think about it, you'll agree that it is far easier to "understand" or discern what's wrong with others than it is to see what is wrong in us. Nonetheless, all of us have what the psalmist calls "secret faults" – things that are wrong with us that aren't readily apparent; or, things that we know about, but protect because they seem easier to live with than to actually deal with and release! At the same time, we also live with the pain of knowing that our lives could be so much fuller and richer were it not for these "secret faults."

The great problem with holding onto hidden faults is that, left unchecked, these spiritual toxins can cripple our walk and slowly kill the life of Christ within us! If we fail to deal with them, they develop into what the psalmist calls, "presumptuous sins" – sins we willfully hold onto and indulge in that ultimately will cause lasting devastation.

So, together we fast. We fast so that God can allow the toxins in our lives to surface, be dealt with, and be healed. We fast so that when the temporary pain and discomfort of spiritual detoxification has passed, we will arise with new power for the days to come! We fast so that we may say with the psalmist, "Let the words of my mouth, and the meditation of my heart, be acceptable in Thy sight, O LORD, my strength, and my redeemer." (Psalm 19: 14 KJV)

TAKE ACTION!

Thoughts for your Journal:
- ➤ Reflect on spiritual toxins (habits, dispositions, tendencies, etc.) you have been struggling with that may be surfacing, even as we begin this Consecration. Write down what it is that you want the Lord to cleanse you from during this time of consecration. What are you willing to do to get them completely out of your system?
- ➤ Over the next three days, write down challenges/toxins that come to the surface in your spirit and surroundings as you deny your flesh. Make a note of what you are expecting to be different in the days to come.

Prayer Focus:
- ➤ Pray that God will give you the discernment to see what is coming to the surface as your spirit is "detoxing" and the wisdom to deal with it.
- ➤ Pray that God will purge and cleanse you from all sins, known and unknown, giving you courage to confront, confess and forsake those things that need to be confessed.
- ➤ Like Daniel, repent not just for yourself, but also for your family, church, community and country for failure to seek the face of God. Pray in faith that God will respond positively to our repentance! (2 Chronicles 7: 14; Daniel 9:4-6).

Suggested Bible Reading:
- ➤ Psalm 19
- ➤ 2 Chronicles 7
- ➤ I John 1

Day Five
Hearing The Father!

Focus Verse: *"My sheep hear My voice, and I know them and they follow me."* (John 10:27 KJV)

When my children were younger, few things infuriated me more, as a parent, than calling them and feeling that I was being ignored. I'm blessed to be the father of young adults who, throughout their lives, have made a consistent and commendable effort to be extremely responsive and respectful to their mother and me. But occasionally it would happen. I'd be in one part of the house trying to get their attention while they were in another room having a "good ol' time." I'd hear them moving about or laughing and talking, and it would "grind my gears" that they couldn't hear me. Usually when I'd finally storm into the room where they were, I'd discover that they simply couldn't hear me over the racket of their own raucous voices, the television, or their music. *Frustrating.* I am sure that our Heavenly Father must feel a similar frustration with us, His children. He hears us moving through life; hears our thoughts and longings; hears our whispered prayers and those that never rise to the level of a whisper. He hears our unspoken aspirations and our frustrations, our joy and our pain, and all the while He is calling out to us, wanting to be involved in our lives. But too often, we can't hear His voice over the din and distraction of our daily lives. Truth be told, the volume settings on most of our lives are out of whack! We need to be "reset" back to the original "Manufacturer's settings."

That's what this journey in fasting and prayer is about: resetting, realigning our lives back to the Creator's original intent. The irony is that we long for answers that only the Father can provide. We long to do something different, to be someone greater, and to go somewhere we have never been. We wonder why we do the things we do - or more precisely, why we do the things we don't want to do. We wonder why we keep attracting people and experiences we don't want and repelling those we desire. We wonder how we can break the negative cycles in our lives. We wonder – and all the while, the Father is speaking and reaching out with the answers and solutions we so desperately crave but can't hear.

This season of fasting and prayer is an opportunity for us to turn down the distractions in our lives and simply be still and know that He is God (Psalm 46: 10). Jesus said, *"My sheep hear my voice..."* (John 10:27) - an assertion that is at once soothing and scary. It is comforting to know that I have a Good Shepherd who cares enough to speak to me, but I am troubled by the deeper implication, that if I can't hear His voice I may not be one of His sheep! When I become still, I realize that for a Christian, hearing the Shepherd is supposed to be the norm, not the rare exception.

We are so "fearfully and wonderfully made" that scientists tell us the average person has 500-700 different skills and abilities - far more than most of us realize. Our brains can store 100 trillion facts. Our minds can handle 15,000 decisions per second –decisions that we don't even know are being made. For example, we don't even think about the processes of digesting the different kinds of foods we eat, but our brain is constantly working in the background, keeping thousands of things going smoothly. We can smell 10,000 different odors. Our touch can detect 1/25,000 of an inch in thickness. And yet with all of this, we can't hear the voice of our Maker, though He is speaking to us daily. When is the last time you heard God and immediately knew it was His voice?

Our problem is sensory overload. In his book, *Hunger for God: Desiring God Through Fasting and Prayer*, John Piper wrote, "If we don't feel strong desires for the manifestation of the glory of God, it is not because we have drunk deeply and are satisfied. It is because we have nibbled so long at the table of the world. Our soul is stuffed with small things, and there is no room for the great. If we are full of what the world offers, then perhaps a fast might express or even increase, our soul's appetite for God. Between the dangers of self-denial and self-indulgence is the path of pleasant pain called fasting."

What is to be done? We need a "reset." We need to adjust the volume levels by stepping away from things we love and allow to monopolize our time – food; television; secular entertainment; social media, more social media, and even more social media; as well as other personal attachments. We need to be honest enough to admit that most of us spend more time eating, watching television and interacting on social media than we do in prayer and the Word of God. Only when we step away from these things, will we realize that they are not only distractions, they are closet addictions.

I like something that my friend, Pastor Timothy Findley said, "We want God to speak louder; God wants us to turn our lives down!" Our flesh will never volunteer for this - it will be difficult, but with God we can do it! I can't say that earnestly seeking God will feel easy, but I can promise, it will be worth it!

TAKE ACTION!

Thoughts for your Journal:

> ➤ When was the last time you heard God speaking to you on a consistent basis? How was your spiritual walk different then than it is now?
> ➤ In what ways do you want your life to be different after this Journey?

Prayer Focus:

> ➤ Pray for the grace to step away from every "closet addiction" in your life so that you will have lasting breakthroughs after this fast is over.
> ➤ Declare and decree that you will receive power and divine directions from the presence of God during this Journey that will positively affect your destiny.
> ➤ Decree in the Name of Jesus that this is your season of permanent breakthroughs and double-portion anointing.

Suggested Bible Reading:

> ➤ Psalm 37
> ➤ I Kings 19:11–13
> ➤ John 10

Day Six
Familiar Voices, New Opportunites

Focus Verse: *"So that thou incline thine ear unto wisdom, and apply thine heart to understanding."* (Proverbs 2:2 KJV)

I will never forget that early spring evening in 1992. At the time, I was serving as Pastoral Assistant in a growing church in Baltimore, MD. My somewhat meager salary afforded me relatively few pleasures. On this particular evening, I had gone to a local restaurant, novel in hand, to enjoy a quiet dinner alone with my thoughts – some "me" time. As I settled comfortably into my seat and placed my order, my reverie was suddenly interrupted by a familiar voice. It was Sharon, one of the newer members from the church, who had taken a part-time job as hostess for the restaurant. Seeing I was alone, she decided to take a few minutes' break just to chat. I wish I could say that I was elated she joined me, but unfortunately, that wouldn't be true. I love people, especially church members, but this was one of those times that I just wanted to be by myself – just me, my Buffalo wings, and my book. I forced my attention away from the book and politely began to listen to what she was saying. That's when my life took a drastic turn for the better.

When I turned my full attention to what she was saying, I realized that the Lord had brought me to that restaurant on that particular night, not so that I could enjoy my book, but so that I might have a chance encounter with an opportunity that I didn't even know existed. She shared that she had taken the hostess job to make a few extra dollars to supplement her income as a Federal Government employee, but that she was going to be leaving the restaurant the following week because she had come across an opportunity to work as a consultant, teaching government workers – a job for which she would be making more money per day than I was making per week in my full-time ministry position.

"Ding! Ding! Ding! Ding!" As I listened, an alarm went off in my spirit and I realized that although I had never worked for the Federal Government, I had the skills, experience and training to do what Sharon was talking about.

Within a couple of weeks, I was a "consultant" – doubling and tripling my weekly salary – working part-time. And the beautiful thing was that it in no way interfered with my ministry at the church!

The point of the story is this: Wisdom is speaking all around us constantly. All that we need to do is "incline" (turn) our ear toward it. When we become true listeners, not just hearers, unbelievable opportunities will come to light. Our memory verse challenges us not only to listen, but to apply our "heart" (mind) to understanding. This implies a focused and active attentiveness. In fact, biblically, this kind of listening suggests obedience. What if I had only listened to my friend's words, but then been too timid to speak up and offer my services?

The wise person listens, learns, and... ACTS! The wise person seeks to understand before seeking to be understood. Wisdom is speaking all around you today. Are you listening?

TAKE ACTION!

Thoughts for your Journal:
- ➤ Reflect on opportunities missed in your life because either you didn't "hear" what the wisdom of God was saying or because you didn't take action.
- ➤ Are there any things that you have recently been hearing in your spirit, but not really listening to and obeying?

Prayer Focus:
Today, ask God to give you a "listening ear" and an obedient heart so that you will never again miss a God-sent opportunity.

Suggested Bible Reading:
- ➤ Proverbs 2
- ➤ Genesis 3 - 5
- ➤ Matthew 2

Day Seven
Holy Curiosity!

Focus Verse: *"And when the Lord saw that he [Moses] turned aside to see, God called unto him out of the midst of the bush, and said, Moses, Moses. And he said. Here am I."* (Exodus 3:4 KJV)

This was a destiny moment for Moses. It was a moment that all of heaven was observing with bated breath. This was the instant for which all of his life heretofore had been preparation. God had orchestrated the staging of this encounter down to the minutest details. No doubt, the Almighty had posted an angel at this one particular shrub, from its germination up until this day of days, to be sure that no desert windstorm would uproot it and no hungry mountain goat would devour it. The divine stage was set. This would be a moment that Moses would never forget; a calling that would be indelibly etched into his consciousness. Finally, after centuries of waiting, the chosen deliverer had been born. After a lifetime of preparation, he who would be known as the "Law-Giver" is ushered onto the scene. The Glory of God alights on the bush. Moses, likely chasing a stray lamb, comes around an outcropping of rock into the mountain clearing. He notices the burning bush as he rushes over to pick up the stray. The host of heaven watches in silence. It's time for God to speak.

But strangely, God draws out the dramatic moment a little further. He doesn't utter a word. He won't. Not until Moses turns aside to see what many men in their busyness, haste, or even in their fear of fire, might have missed – the fact that although the bush is ablaze it is not being consumed. Moses turns aside – God speaks – the rest is history.

I believe God orchestrates such moments of wonder in our lives; times at which He sets the stage to speak to us in extraordinary ways. I can't help but wonder how many of them we miss because we arrive at a phenomenon for which we have no explanation, but instead of "turning aside" to see how it can be – instead of investigating to see if God is hiding somewhere in the mix – we continue on about our business. We have neither the time nor the inclination to "turn aside." We lack what I call "Holy Curiosity." We may even lack the powers of observation to realize that something supernatural is going on.

There are "burning bushes" in each of our lives –things that according to the laws of nature and logic should not exist. The doctor told some of us years ago that we wouldn't make it, or that we would have diminished capacity, yet we are here alive and more well than medical science can account for. We have been through fires that couldn't consume us. We have gone through deep waters, but didn't drown. We have had less and done more with it... need I go on? Could it be that God has been trying to pique our "holy curiosity" – that He has been trying to get our attention so that He can reveal our destiny?

The stage is set. Heaven is watching. Destiny awaits. Will you "turn aside" today to see what God is saying?

Lord, forgive me for the times that I have been too busy to notice or investigate the "burning bush." Open my eyes, Dear Lord. Give me a hearing ear, and an understanding heart. Deliver me from being so busy or jaded that I continue about my business when destiny is trying to call me. In Jesus' Name, Amen.

TAKE ACTION!

Thoughts for your Journal:
- ➤ As you look back over the last year or two, are there any "burning bushes" (sacred moments) that you failed to take time to consider?
- ➤ In light of this devotional thought, what changes might you make in how you look at and approach life?

Prayer Focus:
- ➤ Pray that God will cause you to be more sensitive to His movement in your life and to His voice.

Suggested Bible Reading:
- ➤ Exodus 1 – 3

Fuel Stop
Take Time to Dream

"It doesn't take any more energy to create a big dream than it does to create a little one." – General Wesley Clark

This Journey is more than just spiritual. Fasting and prayer opens us up to divine insight and direction, but it can also bring great focus and clarity in our natural lives. Are you ready for your life – your everyday, natural life – to make a 180-degree turn for the better? Are you ready to be so empowered that you begin to see possibilities where before you had only seen problems? If your answer was "Yes!" then you are ready to create your Dreams List, the beginning point of a successful life blueprint. In a moment I am going to invite you to begin to write your dreams in your journal. This will be important because your Dream List lies at the heart of a successful life blueprint. It is from this list that the plan and discipline of your life will emerge. In writing your Dreams List, you are only limited by your imagination. There is no limit to the number of dreams you may include on your personal Dreams List. Think of this list as the Highlight Reel of your Future Life – the most successful and satisfying life that you can imagine for yourself...a life not affected by your current financial status, family pressures, or even your current level of confidence or competence.

Remember that your Dreams List is not the same as a Goal List, which will come later. It is not a commitment, but rather a way of clarifying exciting possibilities for your future. Upon completion of your Dreams List, you will discover that your mental, physical and emotional energies are refreshed and refocused with laser clarity. The simple act of writing down your dreams will create the feeling that your life has been redirected toward the accomplishment of what is truly important to you. The simple act of writing your dreams will awaken inner excitement about remote possibilities transformed by your imagination into probabilities. Are you ready to dream?

Creating Your Dreams List

➢ Find a quiet time and place where you won't be disturbed for at least thirty minutes.

➢ Create a section in your journal designated as "My Dreams List" and add the current date at the top.

➢ The Dreams List will have three parts:

1. Things you want to DO in your lifetime – list 30 things you would love to Do before you die if you had unlimited time, talent, money, self-confidence, and family support.

2. Things you want to HAVE in your lifetime – list 30 things you would love to HAVE before you die if you had unlimited time, talent, money, etc.

3. Things you want to BE in your lifetime – list 30 things you want to BE before you die if you had unlimited time, talent, money, etc.

➢ Rules: Don't rush. Wait a few minutes if necessary for the ideas to flow. Do not over-analyze the possibilities or probabilities of achieving each dream based on your current life-circumstances. Allow your imagination to run free. Write down everything that comes to mind no matter how silly or outlandish. You can edit later, but for now, get every thought down on paper without mental reservation. There are no limits to a Dreams List. Write them all down.

The beauty of this exercise is that you will discover that the dreams you have taken the time to write down are not just "dreamed up," they were part of you all along. Committing them to paper empowers them to take on new life in your spirit. Over time, you will notice unexpected opportunities arising to achieve even some of what you thought were your most improbable dreams. Of course, it will be up to you to take advantage of those opportunities.

Once you have completed your Dreams List, you will want to review and revise it each year. As you accomplish each dream, record the date on your list. Don't cross it off. The dream with the date of accomplishment will serve as life-long reminders of your God-given power to create and live out a life plan.

Day Eight
Amazing Purpose!

Focus Verse: *"Not as though I had already attained, either were already perfect: but I follow after, if that I may apprehend that for which also I am apprehended of Christ Jesus."* (Philippians 3:12 KJV)

Amazing Grace, how sweet the sound, that saved a wretch like me; I once was lost, but now am found; was blind, but now I see." What a beautiful hymn, one with a message so powerful that even people who don't know the Lord, are familiar with its lyrics. We who have been redeemed never cease to celebrate the amazing grace of God that "looked beyond our faults and saw our needs." God, through Jesus Christ, has given us what we could never earn or deserve. With such an abundance of grace – unmerited favor and enabling power as has been given to us, surely we should all be experiencing lives of victory, power and significance. However, you know as well as I do, that for most of us this is not the case. Why? Well, in a nutshell, because while we have been busy celebrating Grace, we have overlooked her equally beautiful but jealous sister, Purpose. Our reasons are understandable, really. Grace requires nothing of us. Purpose requires everything – she is simply too "high maintenance" for most of our taste. What we fail to see is that when Purpose is understood, loved and embraced, she loves back...lavishly. Those few who take the trouble to "court" and pursue Purpose, often find success and meaning beyond their wildest dreams. Purpose is every bit as amazing as Grace!

One of the criticisms that some "suitors" have raised about Purpose, is that she is a perfectionist, demanding that those who seek her strive for a higher standard than any sensible person could deem reasonable. In our memory verse for today, Paul seems to lend credence to that complaint as he admits, "[It's] not as though I... were already perfect." Like the Apostle, we struggle with that word, "perfect." Let's be clear. The word "perfect" as used in the Bible of humans does not refer to sinless perfection. Old Testament characters described as "perfect" were clearly not sinless. Although various Hebrew and Greek words are translated "perfect," the central thought is usually either "completeness in all details" or "having reached a goal or achieved a purpose." Here in our text, Paul is admitting that he has not yet fully achieved Purpose in God. How refreshing to know that one as great as Paul did not consider himself to have arrived.

But also how challenging it is to observe Paul's single-minded determination to fully apprehend God's Purpose for his life. He says, "I press on to take hold of that [Purpose] for which Christ Jesus has taken hold of me" (NIV). The King James Version uses the word "apprehend." The idea is not just to clasp lightly, but also to accost, to seize in one's grasp. Paul is declaring that his passionate goal in life is to lay hold of and to fulfill Christ's purpose for him. To that end, there is no price too high for him to pay. Is it any wonder then that the Apostle who considered himself to have been "born out of season" and the "least of all," would end up being arguably the greatest New Testament writer? What might happen in our lives if we were to offer God the same degree of single-minded focus on the fulfillment of purpose?

Not long ago, I came across the following words in my study time:

"If you fail or refuse to learn your God-given purpose, your options automatically become: (a) your own personal vision for your life, (b) society's vision for your life, or (c) the devil's vision for your life. With these plans, you may experience great financial success, but in the end, none of these visions will bring you fulfillment, satisfaction or peace of mind (see Proverbs 19: 21)." – Gillis Triplett

Every one of us has a unique God-given purpose. It is our individual responsibility to discover and embrace that purpose (Romans 12: 2). How do we begin? Earnest prayer and waiting in the presence of the Lord must surely be our starting point. All the time, the Father is speaking. Unfortunately, we are often slow to hear. We need to reclaim the lost art of silence – of simply waiting in His presence until He says what He desires to say to us.

Allow me to share just two more pointers from Paul: First, focus on the pursuit of purpose with single-minded determination. Paul says, "...this one thing I do..." (Philippians 3: 13).

This kind of focus requires the stripping away of unnecessary entanglements and activities. Too many of us are hindered in our purpose because we have never learned to prioritize and say, "no." Secondly, Paul teaches us to keep moving, "forgetting those things which are behind...I press toward *the mark..."* (Philippians 3: 13, 14). In our quest for Purpose, we must remember to forget!

Forgetting doesn't mean losing all memory of the past, but moving on and leaving it done and settled. Dwelling on your past – good or bad – will never advance you toward your purpose.

The choice is yours – will you continue to rest complacently in the company of Amazing Grace? Or will we accept her invitation to meet her sister, Amazing Purpose? Purpose is demanding, but oh so worth the trouble.

TAKE ACTION!

Thoughts for your Journal:
➢ Do you know God's unique purpose for your life?
➢ What actions are you taking today and this week toward knowing or fulfilling the purpose of God in your life?

Prayer Focus:
➢ Ask God to reveal His purpose in your life; to show you the specifics of His will for you. What were you uniquely created to do? Pray that He will help you to get about your "Father's business."

Suggested Bible Reading:
➢ Proverbs 24
➢ Psalm 90
➢ Philippians 3

Day Nine
The Longest Four Letter Word!

Focus Verse: *"I beseech you therefore, brethren, by the mercies of God, that you present your bodies a living sacrifice, holy, acceptable unto God, which is your reasonable service"* (Romans 12:1)

In the world of today, "surrender" is a dirty word. We live in the "never let them see you sweat" generation. We are taught "He who loves least has the most power in any relationship." We are instructed to "always look out for 'number one'." And in our current world political climate, concessions are avoided because of the fear of appearing to "wave the white flag of surrender." Is it any wonder then that the old hymn, "I Surrender All," never finds its way onto the "Top Ten" of the Gospel Hit Parade? Even so, in his bestselling book, *The Purpose-Driven Life*, Pastor Rick Warren asserts that surrender to God is the heart of worship. Quite frankly, I am struggling with this idea. I love to sing. I love to lift my hands. I don't mind bowing. The Lord knows, I even enjoy giving. But to suggest that somehow my worship is not complete unless I am willing to totally surrender? That seems a bit far-fetched.

Really, I have no problem with the general idea of surrendering to God as the Lord of the universe...and even as the Lord – in a very general and impersonal way – of my life. My problem comes when He begins to try to carry over that "Lord" business into my personal life. When He begins meddling in my relationships and personal affairs, that's when I struggle with surrender.

I am not even going to lie. I am disturbed by some of the dangerous statements that Warren makes about surrender in his book:

"You know you're surrendered to God when you rely on God to work things out instead of trying to manipulate others, force your agenda, and control the situation."

"You know you're surrendered when you don't react to criticism and rush to defend yourself. Surrendered hearts show up best in relationships. You don't edge others out, you don't demand your rights, and you aren't self-serving when you're surrendered."

"The most difficult area to surrender for many people is their money. Many have thought, "I want to live for God but I also want to earn enough money to live comfortably and retire someday." Retirement is not the goal of a surrendered life, because it competes with God for the primary attention of our lives."

"Genuine surrender says, "Father, if this problem, pain sickness, or circumstance is needed to fulfill your purpose and glory in my life or in another's, please don't take it away."

I am painfully pricked by such statements. And yet I know in my heart of hearts that they are true, that God can only use me when I fully surrender every aspect of my life over to Him.

He can do His greatest work in my life, only when I truly surrender all aspects of that life over to His capable and loving hands. Warren says it like this, "Sometimes it takes years, but eventually you discover that the greatest hindrance to God's blessing in your life is not others, it is yourself – your self-will, stubborn pride, and personal ambition. You cannot fulfill God's purposes for your life while focusing on your own plans."

Father, forgive me for those areas that I am still holding back from the light of Your Lordship. Today, I choose to surrender every area of my life into Your hands. And I will surrender tomorrow, and the next day, and every day until my sacrifice is fully consumed on the altar of Your loving purpose for me. Jesus, I invite you today to be the Lord of every kingdom of my heart. In Jesus' Name, Amen.

TAKE ACTION!

Thoughts for your Journal:
What areas of your life are you holding back from God?

Prayer Focus:
> ➤ Pray that God will help you to surrender every area of your life over to His Lordship.
> ➤ Pray that God will continue His cleansing work in your life and in the church.

Suggested Bible Reading:
➤ Romans 6
➤ Galatians 2
➤ Philippians 2

Day Ten
Renovation for Growth!

Focus Verses: *"Enlarge the place of thy tent, and let them stretch forth the curtains of thine habitations: spare not, lengthen thy cords, and strengthen thy stakes; For thou shalt break forth on the right hand and on the left; and thy seed shall inherit the Gentiles, and make the desolate cities to be inhabited."* (Isaiah 54: 2 - 3 KJV)

Most people renovate and enlarge following growth. In our text today, the people of God are instructed to renovate and enlarge in anticipation of growth. I can't read this text without thinking of how a family that is expecting a new baby prepares the home for the arrival of a new family member. In this text, however, there is no pregnancy, just a promise. I remember a story that is told concerning the healing ministry of the late Smith Wigglesworth, a powerful British evangelist of the early 20th century. Wigglesworth was known as a man of great faith whose methods were sometimes unorthodox, yet he saw many miracles. In one instance, Wigglesworth prayed for a man with no feet. After praying, the evangelist told the man to go to the local boot-maker and buy some shoes. Over the boot-maker's objections, the man told him to put shoes on his stumps. When the boot-maker went to put the shoes on the stumps, brand new lower legs and feet appeared to fit into the shoes, and the man could walk again. I wonder what size shoes the footless man ordered. When he was rolled into the shoe shop, he had a promise, but no growth. Growth only came as a result of preparing for the promise before he could see any evidence of it. His faith became his evidence! (Hebrews 11: 1).

And so, it is in our text. The Lord speaks an incredible promise into an impossible situation. He gives instructions to a woman who is not only barren, but widowed. He tells her to do a "home renovation," enlarging her dwelling place to accommodate miraculous growth. He promises her that He is about to "flip the script;" that she who has been bereaved, barren, exiled and rejected shall soon have more children than the wife who has been in a fruitful marriage all along (Isaiah 54: 1, 3). It is an incredible promise for an impossible situation. But is it practical? Does it make sense? Wouldn't it make more sense to hold off on the expansion project until she is again married and with child – or at least engaged to be married?

The barren woman in the text represents exiled Israel. But I suspect that she also represents you and me as we struggle, at certain points in our lives, to come to grips with God's incredible promises for our impossible situations. The first lesson we must learn is that God's promises and processes may not always practical from our point of view. "*His ways are not our ways...*" (Isaiah 55:8). We say, "I'll believe it when I see it." He says, "You'll see it when you believe it." We say, "I'll expand when the growth comes." He says, "The growth will come when you expand." We say, "I can't afford to tithe or to sow extravagantly." He says, "You can't afford not to tithe and sow extravagantly." His way is not practical, but it is proven.

His Word never falls to the ground. His instructions, when followed, always bring the desired results.

So then, what are His instructions? What is the Lord saying to us today?

Firstly, He is saying that we should praise Him for the promise before we see the provision! *"Sing O barren woman...burst into song, shout for joy"* (Isaiah 54: 1 NIV). In the Near East, barrenness was considered a disgrace, a cause for embarrassment. What a place from which to praise! The challenge to us today is can we praise even in our place of disgrace?

Can you praise even out of your brokenness and embarrassment?

Secondly, He is instructing us to enlarge and renovate our lives before the promise comes to fruition! *"Enlarge the place of your tent, stretch your tent curtains wide, do not hold back; lengthen your cords, strengthen your stakes"* (Isaiah 54: 2 NIV). In other words, we are called to start "living large" (mentally and spiritually) before we become "large." Our thinking needs to change before our address changes. My grandfather used to say, "You have to start the way you expect to end." Some churches and businesses never grow beyond a certain size because they stay stuck in a small mentality – doing things the way a small, struggling church or business would do it. Some people never grow to their potential because they allow themselves to become stagnant, stuck in a comfort zone. I believe that God is calling us to reinvent ourselves; to change our paradigm. He is calling us to "renovate for growth." If we will do the renovation, He will send the augmentation!

TAKE ACTION!

Thoughts for your Journal:

➢ Renovation often requires demolition. What areas of your life is the Holy Spirit saying need to be removed to make room for the growth that God is promising?

➢ Take a few minutes and prayerfully write down the answers to the following questions: o What has God promised you? o What has God promised your family, your community, or your house of worship (in your understanding)? Take time today to praise Him for those promises.

Prayer Focus:

➢ Pray that the Lord will open the "womb" of your spirit, so that you may become spiritually and intellectually fruitful!

➢ Ask Him to give you positive "fruit" that will remain.

➢ Pray that God will help you to enlarge your 'tent' so that you will be ready for the Harvest that He has promised.

Suggested Bible Reading:

➢ Proverbs 26

➢ Isaiah 43: 1-7

➢ Isaiah 54

Day Eleven

The Audacity of Faith:
Embrace the Impossible

Focus Verses: *"Then Elisha said, Hear the word of the LORD; Thus saith the LORD, Tomorrow about this time shall a measure of fine flour be sold for a shekel, and two measures of barley for a shekel, in the gate of Samaria. Then a lord on whose hand the king leaned answered the man of God, and said, Behold, if the LORD would make windows in heaven, might this thing be? And he [Elisha] said, Behold, thou shalt see it with thine eyes, but shalt not eat thereof."* (II Kings 7: 1-2 KJV)

For most of us, the concept of "faith" evokes images of mental gymnastics. We struggle with what it means to have faith in God. Is faith something we can feel? Is it a sense of total certainty without doubt or fear? Is faith an inner calm devoid of confusion or chaos? Is it a philosophical or psychological positioning of the mind through which we can overcome our circumstances? Is it a mental mantra, the repeating of which enables one to manipulate the Eternal? What is faith, and how do I appropriate it to bring about results in my life? I think that the simplest and best definition is, "faith is the Word of God believed and obeyed." Three vital concepts – the Word of God, Belief, and Obedience– form the essential tripod upon which faith can stand. If any of the three is missing, there is no faith. Without a "Word" there can be no faith, for what would there be to hear, believe and obey? From Genesis to Revelation, every hero of faith moved in obedience to a "Word."

It occurs to me that much of what we call "faith" now is a manufactured thing, lacking life or substance. We call ourselves stepping out in faith, but we have no Word – written or oral – from God upon which to base it. Then we become disenchanted with God when our "air castles" waver and crash to the ground. Faith requires a "Word," a divine promise claimed through belief and obedience. It also goes without saying that there can be no faith without the vital element of Belief, but what of obedience?

Too often we fail to see our faith become reality because although we have a "Word," and although we believe it, we refuse to get up and obey the directions that accompany the promise. Abraham could never have become the father of the faithful, if he had stayed in his father's land and waited on the promise to come to him. His faith was proven by his walk. And so it is today. If we truly believe the promise of God we will move with expectation toward it.

Faith requires a certain audacity, a boldness to step out on what may appear to be improbable promises. Faith requires the audacity to move forward in spite of fears and misgivings. We tend to function on the basis of what we can feel and see. I, for one, will confess here and now that for years I have struggled in the exercise of faith to get the feelings right – that is, to feel absolute certainty that what I am believing (or maybe just hoping) for will indeed come to pass. Lately, I am becoming increasingly convinced that faith in God has little to do with how I feel, and absolutely nothing to do with how things look.

I think that our focus verses bear this out. In the middle of what may well have been the worst famine in the history of Samaria, a prophet named Elisha had the audacity to tell the king and his counselors that "by tomorrow about this time" everything will be different! The promise goes forth that within a day's time, the besieged and wretched population of Samaria would go from starvation to surfeit, from poverty to plenty, from desperation to deliverance. In a single day, hopelessness would be banished, replaced by joy.

To understand how far-fetched this sounds, we need to revisit the facts of their situation. Not only was there famine in the city, there was an overwhelming army outside. Things had gotten so bad that the inhabitants of Samaria – in total disregard of the Pentateuchal laws of uncleanness – were not only eating donkeys, but were paying exorbitant amounts for the least edible part of the donkey, the head (II Kings 6: 25). Some were even resorting to cannibalism (v. 28). The king is at wit's end as he surveys the shambles that his kingdom has become, helpless to help. There is no food to be had. There is no farming to be done, no hunting, no foraging; the enemy is encamped in the fields around the city.

How strange the words of Elisha seem to our rational modern minds, when he proclaims that "by tomorrow about this time" everything will be turned around. Impossible. There was no possible, visible way for enough food to arrive within a day to turn the situation so decisively. It was beyond the ability of human logistics to make it happen. In frustration one of the key advisors to the king explodes. Who does this shaggy, unkempt prophet think he is anyway? "Look, even if the Lord should open the floodgates of the heavens, could this happen?" In other words, he is saying, "Elisha, get real. Don't come in here bringing false hope. I am not feeling this prophecy!"

What the king's advisor failed to consider was that he was not discounting the words of Elisha, but the Word of the Lord! Faith must have an object to which to anchor - the Anchor, the Object, the Author and Finisher of our faith, the Limitless One – the One who cannot lie. How you or I feel – afraid, uncertain, doubtful, hopeful, sure – none of that really matters. He only requires that we have the audacity to believe in the One who promised, and to act accordingly, even if it means embracing the impossible. In the case of those who heard Elisha's prophecy, all that was required was to show up the next day at the gate of the city. They only had to show up – nothing was said about how they were to feel!

How often we feel that we are in the dark. We are at our wit's end. We have exhausted our means and can't see the possibility of rescue. After all, we are surrounded by an army of adversaries who don't play by the same rules, or believe as we believe. But God sees what we don't see. He can create a way where there is no way. He is not bound by our impossibilities. He can do *"exceeding, abundantly above all that we ask or think"* (Ephesians 3:20). God is not even bound by our timetables. He can fix decades-long messes in moments. One of the ways that we can be confident that our deliverance is a result of divine intervention is that it will come about in impossible ways. Our challenge is to embrace the impossible promise of God!

I submit to you that the royal advisor, who discounted the words of Elisha, wouldn't have died if only he had kept his misgivings to himself. *"Life and death are in the power of the tongue...*" (Proverbs 18:21). Surely you don't believe that this advisor to the king was the only skeptic that day. Faith is not the absence of doubt. It is obedience in the face of doubt. Faith is not the absence of fear. It is embracing God's "promise" in spite of personal fears. Faith is trusting God enough to do as He says. That's all.

I don't know what hopeless situation you are facing. I don't know what far-fetched "word" you are struggling to believe and obey. But I want to tell you that no matter how bad it looks, God can turn it around in a day. He can. With man it may be impossible, but with God all things are possible (Luke 1:37). Have the audacity to embrace the impossible promise of God. Show up at the appointed time and place and prepare to be surprised by joy!

TAKE ACTION!

Thoughts for your Journal:
  - ➢ What impossible situations are you facing now?
  - ➢ What promise do you have from the Lord concerning your situation? What   instructions do you have?

Prayer Focus:
  - ➢ Ask God to help you to look beyond the logic of your hopeless situation and keep your eyes on Him.
  - ➢ Pray that He'll help you to realize that faith is not about what you feel or think, but about what you hear (from Him – His Word to you), and your response.
  - ➢ Declare that through your steadfast obedience to Him you will lay hold on every promise He has made.

Suggested Bible Reading:
  - ➢ Proverbs 2
  - ➢ II Kings 6-7
  - ➢ Hebrews 11

Day Twelve
Disturbing God's Rest!

Focus Verses: " _I have set watchmen upon thy walls, O Jerusalem, which shall never hold their peace day nor night: ye that make mention of the LORD, keep not silence, And give Him no rest, till He establish, and till He make Jerusalem a praise in the earth._" (Isaiah 62: 6, 7)

I, for one, struggle with this whole issue of persistence in prayer. To keep asking God for the same thing over and over, seems to me to be an insult to Divine Intelligence and an admission of my own lack of faith. The Scriptures clearly teach that God knows what we need before we even ask (Matthew 6: 8), and that if we pray in faith, we can expect even mountains to be removed (Mark 11: 22 - 24). I have heard and read the words of leading proponents of the "faith movement" who seem to give voice to my sentiments. They say that if you truly believe God, pray and ask for what you will and don't ask any more, but instead, just thank Him for having already done it. Why then, does it seem as if we are enjoined time and time again in scripture to keep persistently praying about unanswered petitions? In Luke 18: 1 - 8, the

Lord goes as far as to compare the believer's perseverance in prayer to the persistence of a widow petitioning and unjust judge. The lesson seems to be that if an unworthy judge – one who feels no constraint of right or wrong – is compelled by persistence to deal justly with a helpless individual, how much more will our righteous God answer the persistent prayers of His children! The entire purpose of the parable is to teach us to pray without giving up (Luke 18: 1).

Praying without giving up. Persistent prayer. I sometimes wrestle with it, because this kind of importunate prayer brings to mind the unrelenting appeals of a whining, spoiled child determined to get his way at all costs. Today's text from Isaiah, however, permanently dispels that image, for here we see why persistence in prayer is a pleasing thing to God.

God says, "I have set watchmen upon thy walls...which shall never hold their peace..." These prophetic watchmen have been stationed on the walls for the primary purpose of waiting and watching for evidence of the Lord's return to and restoration of Zion (Isaiah 52: 8 - 9), but here in our text they are given two other specific and essential activities: a) they are to allow themselves no rest ("to keep not silent") as they continually cry out for the restoration of Jerusalem; and b) they are to give God no rest until He establishes and makes Jerusalem a "praise" in the earth.

As I read this text, a light bulb comes on and I realize that persistent prayer is not about "twisting God's arm" to get Him to do something that He doesn't want to do; it is all about coming to an ultimate level of agreement with His "passionate" intent. We persistently pray for what we already know God has promised to do (Isaiah 62: 1 - 4). In so doing, we demonstrate to God that we desire Him to do a thing as much as He desires to do it. Two simple, perhaps even silly examples come to mind.

First example: Some years ago on my daughter Sharon's 11th birthday, her sole birthday request was for a family outing to Six Flags Over Georgia, the famous amusement park. With game faces, rumbling stomachs, and aching heads, her mom and I (along with her two brothers) strapped ourselves into "thrill" ride after "thrill" ride. Several times as we waited warily for a ride to begin, our teenaged ride- operator would amuse himself/herself by challenging all of us that if we were really ready for the "fun" to begin, we needed to shout our "enthusiasm." Although in each instance my shouts lacked the conviction of the younger riders, the general idea being communicated was clear – the ride-operators wanted us to demonstrate that we indeed wanted them to do what they all along intended to do, start the ride.

Second example – this one is nearer to my heart. In the African American preaching tradition, it is not uncommon to hear preachers elicit a desired audience response with words like – "Somebody tell me to go ahead!" or "I wish someone would tell me to preach!" I am guilty of doing this, so let me speak for myself. Without exception, every time that I have said this, I already fully intended to "preach." But I have found that the entire experience is immensely more satisfying for all involved when the congregation demonstrates that they want to hear what I came to say as much as I want to say it. In fact, I will venture further to say that my ability to preach is magnified and enhanced by the excited, vocal agreement of the congregation.

It is from this perspective, then, that we come to appreciate the value of persevering, persistent prayer. God invites us to labor with Him in the manifestation of His promise in our lives. What an opportunity! We are buckled in for the ride of our lives, but before it can start, God challenges us to show Him that we are as ready for the thrill of fulfilled purpose as He is. Do we truly long for transformation and restoration, or are we just going through the motions? God already knows that which we often fail to discern or admit – the real state of our ardor and enthusiasm toward Him.

When I read these verses from Isaiah, I am convicted anew by the divine invitation to demonstrate the intensity of my desire for God through my consistency and fervency in prayer. Maybe the image of a determined child coming to his parent is not so far from the mark. No one is more shamelessly relentless than a child with a promise from her parent. A child with a promise is impassioned to the point of pressing beyond his own weariness; he doesn't "keep silence." A child with a promise is emboldened to the point of giving her parent "no rest."

Today, we are the heirs to great and precious promises from our Father. Will you come into agreement with His desire to fulfill His promises in your life? Are you childlike enough to continually cry out to Him? Are you determined enough to "give Him no rest"? Jesus said, *"...unless you change and become like little children, you will never enter the kingdom of heaven"* (Matthew 18: 2, NIV). Well, since He put it that way, I think that I will accept my new role as "God's spoiled brat." I will "give Him no rest" until I experience the transformation and restoration that He has promised! Will you join me?

TAKE ACTION!

Thoughts for your Journal:
- ➤ Are there any promises that God has yet to fulfill in your life because your desire and His intentions are not in agreement?
- ➤ The "proof" of desire is in the "pursuit," what does your pursuit of the things of God say about your level of passion for the things of God?
- ➤ In what area are you being challenged today to be shamelessly persistent in prayer?

Prayer Focus:
- ➤ Pray that God will teach you to have a childlike obsession with seeking & crying out continually for everything He has promised you.
- ➤ Ask that He forgive the times that you have "fainted" (given up) concerning things that you know He promised you.

Suggested Bible Reading:
- ➤ Proverbs 30
- ➤ Isaiah 62
- ➤ Luke 18

Day Thirteen
Lessons from a Dry Creek Bed

Focus Verse: *"And it came to pass after a while, that the brook dried up, because there had been no rain in the land."* (I Kings 17:7)

Can you imagine the entries in Elijah's diary as he sat next to a disappearing brook in a place called Cherith? "Cherith - Day 435 – Brook down by two more inches this morning. Barely a trickle remains. Soon it will be completely dry. What will I do next? Don't know where to go – still a "Wanted Man." Inclined to think I may have missed God, but what about the ravens? They still keep showing up morning and evening, like clockwork, delivering my meals. Is this where my journey will end, here at this drying brook? Will Cherith be my final stop?" Elijah's dilemma is like a lot of ours. He finds himself sitting in a place that once sustained him, but now is drying up. To be more specific, he is in a place where God sent him, but where there is no longer living water there. His question is ours: "What do we do when 'the brook' dries up?" What do we do when things, places, or associations that once nurtured us lose their ability to keep us going?

There are several options. Some people stay till the bitter end and die beside "the brook," because that is where God sent them. I have seen people in dying ministries, still fighting for positions and titles. In the words of one of my mentors, that is like fighting for first-class passage on a sinking ship. There are people who believe that once God speaks to give direction, He never changes His directives. They have God figured out – "If he sent me here, and the brook is drying up, He either intends to revive the brook, or this is where I am to die. Admirable, but narrow. The fact that God said, "Go," doesn't mean He meant stay forever. The God of Elijah defies being placed in a box.

Unpredictable, Indefinable, Ineffable – all of these are part and parcel of who God is. He defies definition and constriction. The moment you think you have Him all figured out, that you know which way He is coming, He sweeps in from another direction – entirely out of sync with our expectation and urgency – strangely right on time. He is the Wild God – untamed, undomesticated and seemingly unreliable. But He remains consistent in His compassion, yet predictably providential – a divine paradox.

In other words, the thing that is most predictable about God is that if He sends us to a "brook" that dries up, He always has another Word to direct us to the next place. The problem is not with God's communication abilities, but with our willingness to listen and hear what He is saying. God told Elijah to go to the Brook Cherith. God told the ravens to bring him meals by "airmail." God also told the elements not to rain and the brook to dry up. Is it a hard thing to believe that a God, with a proven track record of sustaining His prophet, would have another direction for him when the brook dried up?

What do you do when your "brook" dries up? Some people take matters into their own hands and start a water conservation program, or they try to pipe in water from the next town over. I think that God laughs at our attempts to fix things on our own. We tend to figure that if we just "do something different" everything will be all right. That depends on the nature of the problem. When it is a God-decreed drought, no amount of water conservation will fix it. When it is a God-ordained drought, our efforts at piping water in from elsewhere are doomed to fail. When it is a God-determined drought, our efforts at fixing things are like treating brain tumors with Tylenol. The answer is not to overcome "dried brook syndrome," but to *be still and know that God is God"* (Psalm 46:10). There is a time for doing, but there is also a time to be quiet, to waiting, and to "know."

What do you do when your "brook" dries up? Sit there and die – praying for a miracle that is not coming? Take matters into our own hands and "fix" the situation? Or do you get still and listen for the next word of direction?

TAKE ACTION!

Thoughts for your Journal:
➤ What "brooks" have dried up in your life?
➤ In what ways have you not been open to the next Word of God for your life?

Prayer Focus:
➤ Today ask that the Father help you to recognize those places in your life that He has allowed to dry out so that your focus would once again be totally upon Him.
➤ Pray that He will help you to be able and willing to move to the next place of sustenance He has ordained in your development.

Suggested Bible Reading:
➤ Proverbs 16
➤ Psalm 127
➤ I Kings 17

Day Fourteen
Dry Creek Beds II: Finding A Place Called "There"!

Focus Verses: *"And it came to pass after a while, that the brook dried up, because there had been no rain in the land. And the word of the LORD came to him, saying, Arise get thee to Zarephath...and dwell there: behold I have commanded a widow woman there to sustain thee."* (I Kings 17:7-9 KJV)

Yesterday, we focused on the pain of seeing places that once sustained us dry up. How do we handle the discomfort of finding ourselves in a place where we believe God sent us, but in which things are no longer flowing as they once did? What do we do when the "brook" dries up? What do we do when things, places, or associations that once nurtured us are no longer able to keep us going? If you are like me, you struggle with accepting the fact that God does send His servants to brooks that dry up. This bothers us because it flies in the face of the much-touted immutability of God – the fact that He is unchanging. God never changes. He never makes mistakes. His counsel forever stands. So then why does He send us to "brooks" that "dry up?" Could it be that He does so to teach us some deeper lessons about who He is? If our "brooks" never "dry up," we might go on thinking that we have God all figured out, that we have Him "tamed," and contained in our hip pocket.

While it is certainly true that God's nature never changes, it is equally true that His directives may change from moment to moment. Most of us don't like this. We long to be settled in one place; to live within the secure boundaries of our comfort zone. God, on the other hand, relishes the journey as much as the final destination. For it is on the journey that we learn dependence, trust, and obedience. It is on our journey with God that we grow. Each place along the way is an opportunity for Him to impart to us a new level of faith.

Our desire for stability can cause us to stay on in places where God once blessed us, long after the "brook" has "dried up" and the cloud of glory has departed. We stay too long, to our own detriment. We rely on ourselves or our circumstances for our survival instead of God. We become guilty of a form of idolatry. We place more faith in the drying "brooks" than in the living God who desperately longs to order our steps to the next place of blessing and growth. The result? We become as stagnant and bitter as the last remaining puddles that we revere and struggle to preserve.

Why does God allow our "brooks" to "dry up?" Perhaps it is to break our attachment; to cause us to realize that our source is not a "brook," or a raven or even a widow woman, but rather the God of Abraham. Our sustenance comes not from the water in a "brook" or even the bread in a raven's mouth or a widow's oven, but from the Word of our God.

Why does God allow "brooks" to dry up? Because the sweet babble of the "brook" can lull us into a comfortable complacency that soon stifles the sound of Heaven. I confess; I don't pray and fast nearly as much when things are easy and certain as I do when the "bottom" drops out. When at ease, we tend to lose our urgency to hear His voice and to seek His direction. So, for the sake of our destiny, God sometimes allows the "brook" to dry up.

We ascribe far too much significance to our "brook," anyway. It was after the brook had dried up that Elijah again heard the Voice that had spoken to him previously telling him to – *"Get thee hence... and hide thyself by the brook Cherith... And it shall be, that thou shalt drink of the brook; and I have commanded the ravens to feed thee there"* (I Kings 17: 3-4 NKJV). Now, as he listens he hears a fresh Word: *"Arise, get thee to Zarephath... and dwell there: behold I have commanded a widow woman there to sustain thee"* (verse 9).

There is a powerful revelation in these verses if we would but grasp it. Elijah's survival and success was never tied to the brook or to the ravens or to the widow. His survival was totally tied to the commandment of the Lord. Note in both of these passages that God says "I have commanded...there..." Wherever God sends His prophet, wherever He sends us is "there" – a place of commanded blessing!

So what do we do when our "brook" dries up? Listen and look for the next "there."

TAKE ACTION!

Thoughts for your Journal:
- ➤ Have you ever been guilty of attaching more importance to a "brook" that God used do sustain you than to the One Who commands your blessings?
- ➤ Why is it difficult to leave our "dried up brooks"?
- ➤ Can you think of any instances where you moved in sync with God to the next "there" in your life? What was the result?

Prayer Focus:
- ➤ Ask forgiveness for the times you have been guilty of spiritual idolatry, worshipping places and associations and people more than God.
- ➤ Determine today to obey His voice no matter where it may lead you.
- ➤ Determine not to miss your next season because of reluctance to leave the familiar boundaries of your comfort zone.

Suggested Bible Reading:
- ➤ Proverbs 23
- ➤ Joshua 1
- ➤ I Kings 18

Tap into the Power of Goals!

"If you want to be happy, set a goal that commands your thoughts, liberates your energy and inspires your hopes." -Andrew Carnegie – The richest man in America in the early 20th century

G oals have been defined as "experiences you have not yet had; places you have not yet been; people you have not yet met; a level of income you have not achieved; a type of relationship you are not now enjoying; or having something you don't currently own" (Charles J. Givens, *Superself*). Goals are the stepping stones to dreams. They are specific, measurable results that are to be produced at a set time in the future.

Do you have goals? Are they written? In the book, *What They Don't Teach You in the Harvard Business School*, Mark McCormack tells of a 1979 study conducted on students in the Harvard MBA program. In that year, the students were asked, *"Have you set clear, written goals for your future and made plans to accomplish them?"* Eighty-four percent had no specific goals at all. Thirteen percent had goals, but they were not in writing. Only three percent of the graduates had written goals and plans.

Ten years later, the members of the class were again interviewed, and the findings, while somewhat predictable, were nonetheless astonishing. The 13 percent of the class who had goals were earning, on average, twice as much as the 84 percent who had no goals at all. And what about the three percent who had clear, written goals? They were earning, on average, ten times as much as the other 97 percent put together – the power of goals.

Experts on the science of success will tell you that the brain is a goal-seeking "machine." When you embrace a clear, specific, measurable goal your subconscious mind is unleashed to work day and night to bring it about. In order to maximize the power of your subconscious mind, your goals must meet two criteria: they must be stated in a way that anyone can measure them; and they must each have specific time and dates attached.

Goals are not expectations. In fact, if what we hope to achieve in life is based on our expectations, we stand to be disappointed. Expectations have to do with how you think others should act, and what the world or life "owes" you. Living by our expectations will almost always result in a large amount of grief, but working to reach established goals will result in great amounts of satisfaction and success. In order to win in life, we must develop goals and drop expectations. Our goals won't just magically come to pass because we deserve them, or because we are entitled to success because of some past suffering. We must develop them, review them and work to reach them.

Goals are not merely good ideas. When goals are not clear and measurable, they become simply wants, wishes, preferences or good ideas. To say that you want to own a new home is a good idea. To state the style, the square footage, the area and the date by which you intend to own it – that's a goal. To say that you intend to lose weight is a good idea. To state how many pounds you are going to lose by a specific date – that's a goal. Got it?

Remember that goals are the incremental steps to your dreams. They are signposts along the way to your dreams. It's no fun to only have long-term goals that take ten years or more to achieve. Start with smaller short-term goals and work up, but keep the big picture in mind.

Corporate coaches have coined an acronym for the kinds of goals that are most effective. They are called S.M.A.R.T. Goals:

➢ **Specific** – clear, concise and simple

➢ **Measurable** – this answers the question of "how much?"

➢ **Achievable** – incremental, not so vast that they can't be achieved in a   prescribed time period

➢ **Realistic** – in keeping with true desires and ambitions

➢ **Timetable** – having milestones and completion dates

Goal-Setting Activity

Do some goal-setting in the following areas or in categories of your own that are important to you:

Spirituality – Which priorities do you have for your walk with God – including your prayer life, Bible study habits, church attendance and service, and soul winning?

➢ **Family** – How can you improve your relationships with spouse, children, and extended family?

➢ **Career** – What do you want achieve from your career?

➢ **Financial** – What do you want to earn? How will you make it happen?

➢ **Education** – What skills will you need to achieve your goals?

➢ **Physical** – Are there health goals that you want to achieve?

➢ **Avocation** – Do you have a hobby that is important to you?

➢ **Service** – How will you make a difference in your community?

Remember that success is nothing more than the progressive, timely achievement of goals. The more specific and measurable your goals are, the more quickly your subconscious mind will be able to identify, locate, and attract the necessary resources for their achievement. To that end, in writing down your goals, avoid subjective words and phrases like: A lot, More, Most, Much, Less, Greater, Fewer, Better or Highest. Subjective words such as these result in nonspecific, ineffective goals. It is not an effective goal, for example, to say: "I intend to lose a lot of weight over the next six months."

Finally, once you have written down your goals – great and small – the next step on your journey toward successfully achieving them is to review your list of goals at least two to three times each day. If possible, read the list out loud with passion and enthusiasm, one goal at a time. Visualize them as already accomplished. As you do this daily, you will activate the power of desire, causing your brain to strive to close the gap between the envisioned goals and your current reality!

Where will you be ten years from now? Chart that course through your goals!

Day Fifteen
Acquired Tastes

Focus Verses: *"O taste and see that the LORD is good: blessed is the man that trusteth in Him. O fear the LORD, ye His saints: for there is no want to them that fear Him."*
(Psalm 34: 8, 9 KJV)

Anyone who has struggled with being overweight knows that the hardest thing about sticking with most diet plans is a simple, five-letter word: "Taste." Why can't what's good for us be good to us, also? The fact of the matter is that if eating were only about fueling our bodies, none of us would be fat. After all, even most skinny people know that eating can be a joy... if the food tastes good. What we often fail to consider, though, is that most tastes are acquired. What one person enjoys might be extremely distasteful to another. Babies, after all, survive and thrive on what we as adults would consider rather bland and boring fare. No self-respecting adult I've ever met has admitted to having a taste or craving for baby food! By the time we are out of diapers, our tastes in food and in other things have begun to develop and become increasingly refined and personal to us.

Of course, "taste" is so much more than merely a biological concept. It speaks of anything for which we have developed a desire or a craving. As with food, we fallen human beings tend to desire things in life that are good to us, but ultimately not good for us. Born in sin, we effortlessly acquire the "taste" for sinful behaviors of all kinds. And to tell the truth, even after we're born again, we struggle with our "taste for sin." You struggle. I struggle. We all struggle with desires and cravings that are destructive to our very souls. Anyone who claims otherwise is a liar or in denial (I John 1: 8). The truth that many of us, even the most seasoned saints, are afraid to tell, is that sin does have pleasure... even if only for a season (Hebrews 11: 25b).

Anyone who has ever struggled for victory over a compulsive or habitual sin knows what it is to agonize over the corrupt cravings that lie at the root of our "indiscretions" - our "taste" for sin. What's a Christian to do? Do we continue in our past sinful lifestyles hoping that God's grace will cover us? God forbid! (See Romans 6: 1, 2). The good news is that although we may have a "taste" for sin, we are able by the grace of God to acquire new and better tastes.

How is this done? It's quite simple, really. It's actually the same process that has been perfected by parents from every part of the planet since time immemorial to introduce children to a hearty diet. Old tastes die as a result of two things: 1) Exposure to new and better tastes; 2) Withdrawal from old inferior tastes. Note that this only works if done in the proper order. Attempting to abandon the old tastes, without having first tasted the new is a sure recipe for failure.

The psalmist says, "O taste and see that the LORD is good..." (Psalm 34: 8). It's an invitation to a Divine taste test. The Almighty says, "You've tried the best that satan has to offer, now try Me." Because we have lived beneath our privilege for so long, walking close to God is an acquired taste. But it's a rich one! The more we "taste" of His goodness, the more we experience His grace, the more we want of Him – and the more distasteful we find our old habits to be. To know God, is to love Him. As we experience intimacy with God, we discover that there are undeniable, irresistible, inalienable benefits derived from delighting in His presence - "...*Blessed is the man that trusts in Him...there is no want to them that fear Him*" (Psalm 34: 8b, 9b). Now this is the ultimate addiction - one with benefits!

As we cultivate our craving for God, we must also choose to withdraw (by the power of His Holy Spirit) from the sinful behaviors and habits that have held us enthralled. Tasting the goodness of the Lord Jesus Christ empowers us to walk away from our old cravings. The propaganda of the enemy is that continual sinning is inevitable; but the promise of God is that He will never allow a temptation to come so strong that we can't resist it! (I Corinthians 10: 13). For children of God who are walking in the Spirit, temptations are simply tests of our character to show us where are hearts are. We discover that as we walk in the Spirit we need no longer fulfill the lusts of the flesh (Galatians 5:16). The cravings for the old lifestyle lose their appeal and slowly leave altogether.

What causes the natural appetite to change? Our appetite changes when we discover something that tastes or makes us feel significantly better than what we were previously consuming. I have learned in past efforts to improve my eating habits, that when I begin to experience the benefits of eating right, I crave the right foods.

Further, I have noticed that when I have removed certain unhealthy foods from my diet, gradually, I no longer missed their taste. The power of the addiction was broken.

Some time back I saw a poster that I've never forgotten. It was in a physician's office of all places. I turned my head and there in full color was the picture of a very fit individual with this caption: "Nothing tastes as good as it feels to be thin." As a person who struggles with my weight, I was impacted by – "Nothing tastes as good as it feels to be thin." We should all want to be better. We should long to do better in our walk with God and in life. I have thought of those words in a spiritual context: No sin, no habit, no self-indulgence "tastes" as good as it feels to be free. "O taste and see...!"

TAKE ACTION!

Thoughts for your Journal:
- ➤ Reflect on what things you have struggled with a habitual "taste" for. At those times when you gave into the temptation, were you consistently, passionately pursuing God?
- ➤ Write down the ways in which you can be more consistent in your pursuit of God.

Prayer Focus:
- ➤ Pray that God will allow you to experience Him in such a way that you will become addicted to Him.
- ➤ Pray that God will show you His sufficient Grace to overcome temptations.

Suggested Bible Reading:
- ➤ Psalm 34
- ➤ Psalm 63
- ➤ Isaiah 55
- ➤ John 4: 1-14

Day Sixteen
Driven...or Led?

Focus Verses: *"That we henceforth be no more children, tossed to and fro, and carried about with every wind of doctrine, by the sleight of men, and cunning craftiness, whereby they lie in wait to deceive..."* (Ephesians 4:14 KJV)

"For as many as are led by the Spirit of God, they are the sons of God." (Romans 8:14 KJV)

Most of us struggle through life with doing the right thing. Christianity raises the standard. We are taught by the Savior, not only to do the right thing, but to do it for the right reasons. Reasons or motives are difficult and tricky things. They can have us going in the wrong direction even while it feels like we are doing everything right! You remember the old adage, "The road to hell is paved with good intentions." It's true. The sad reality is that the majority of professing Christians are more emotion-driven than we are Spirit-led. Too often, we live, serve, pray, give, and worship according to the dictates of how we feel more than according to the leadership of the Holy Spirit or the principles of the Word of God.

How do we know if we are emotion driven rather than Spirit-led?

➤ Emotion-driven follow the standards at work or at school, but always feel that they should get an exemption – based on how they are feeling or what they are currently experiencing – from following the standards God's Word.

➤ Emotion-driven people get their doctrine and theology from Facebook more than from the "Good Book."

➤ Emotion-driven people feel "anointed" to preach or minister in the pulpit, but not to study or make it to prayer meetings, church cleanup, Bible Class or ministerial training. If they show up, they come late or leave early.

➤ Emotion-driven people feel let down by life, people, God, the church and the pastor, but never by their own disobedience. They never make a connection between their disobedience or incomplete obedience and their difficulties.

➤ Emotion-driven people are great scorekeepers and will justify their failures by comparing the failures of others.

The dangers of being emotion- driven instead of Spirit-led:

1. The Danger of Doing the Right Thing for the Wrong Reasons - When we allow our emotions to sit in the "driver's seat," we find ourselves doing things that we should do, but from the wrong heart-orientation. We serve to be seen or appreciated by man rather than God. We run the risk of being lifted up in pride or of placing public approval above integrity. If we allow emotions to drive us, we will find ourselves ignoring our internal wretchedness because of our external goodness. Jesus warned in Matthew 7:22-23, that in the final judgment there will be many who will profess to have done many good works in His name, only to be rejected from entrance into the Kingdom. Doing the right things from the wrong motives inevitably leads us away from God.

2. The Danger of Doing the Wrong Thing That FEELS Right - One of the dangers of trusting our emotions is that they are deceitful. Based on circumstances and stimuli, we can be misled into doing wrong because it feels right. Emotions can cause us to confuse revenge with justice, to confuse lust with love, and to confuse selfish ambition with service to God. Jeremiah was certainly correct when he said that the *"The heart is deceitful above all things, and desperately wicked: who can know it?"* (Jeremiah 17:9). Emotions are an unreliable moral compass, because they recognize no ultimate standard, no true north.

3. The Danger of Inconsistency. Emotion-driven people can't be counted on over the long haul because their function is bound to their feelings. Paul said it best in our focus verse from Ephesians 4:14, when we are emotion-driven we are like children "tossed" on the prevailing winds of sentiment and circumstance. Emotion-driven people can only be counted on to do what they feel like doing. Emotion-driven people come to church when they feel like it, pray only when guilt or desperation drives them to their knees and serve only when there is a chance to be seen. They can only be as consistent as their emotions.

To remain emotion-driven is to lead a life of perpetual natural and spiritual immaturity. We are born again as children of God, but we are called to become Sons of God – there is a difference. A "child" must be entrusted to babysitters and schoolmasters. A "son" is one who has matured enough to be entrusted with authority in the household. *"As many as are led by the Spirit of God, they are the sons of God"* (Romans 8:14).

When we are Spirit-led, we grow in grace and the knowledge of Jesus Christ. When we are Spirit-led, we find ourselves becoming daily more like Him. When we are Spirit-led, we consistently do the right things for the right reasons - even at the cost of our comfort! When we are Spirit-led, our lives become living sacrifices. We no longer are focused on anyone else's behavior other than the example of the Author and Finisher of our Faith, Christ Jesus. When we are Spirit-led, we find life, joy and peace, even in the midst of the trials and turmoil of earthly life.

What's driving you? Are you emotion-driven or Spirit-led?

TAKE ACTION!

Thoughts for your Journal:
- Reflect on your life and service to the Lord. In what areas of your spiritual walk have you been more emotion driven than Spirit-led?
- Ask the Holy Spirit for insight and write down any areas in which you have.... a) done the right thing for the wrong reasons; b) done the wrong things because it felt right at the time; c) been inconsistent because of how you felt.
- Write down any areas in which you know that you have not been obedient or have rendered incomplete obedience to the leadership of the Holy Spirit in your life.

Prayer Focus:
- Ask God to grant you the gift of true repentance and amendment of your ways.
- Pray that God will make you sensitive to hear and consistently follow His voice in your life.
- Pray that God will complete a lasting work in your life as a result of this journey.

Suggested Bible Reading:
- Ephesians 4
- I Corinthians 2: 1 – 3: 3
- Galatians 5

Day Seventeen
The Yoke Destroyer!

Focus Verses: *"And it shall come to pass in that day, that his burden shall be taken away from off thy shoulder, and his yoke from off thy neck, and the yoke shall be destroyed because of the anointing."* (Isaiah 10:27 KJV)

I love the old hymn, "Jesus Breaks Every Fetter." It reminds me of the compassion and power of our Savior; that He is willing and able to do away with every hindrance that seeks to hold me back from my destiny. "Jesus breaks every fetter and He sets me free!" He completely saves! In today's focus verse, we are allowed "ringside" seats at the spectacle of deliverance. We are reminded, through the example of His dealings with Israel, that the Lord's chastening is not forever. The promise is that at the appointed time, He will turn the tables on the enemy and completely deliver His chosen ones. Listen to the Lord's assurance to His people –

"Therefore, this is what the Lord, the Almighty, says: 'O my people who live in Zion, do not be afraid of the Assyrians, who beat you with a rod and lift up a club against you, as Egypt did. Very soon

my anger against you will end and my wrath will be directed to their destruction. The Lord Almighty will lash them with a whip... In that day their burden will be lifted from your shoulders, their yoke from your neck; the yoke shall be broken...' "[emphasis added] (Isaiah 10: 24-27a, NIV).

Oh, if only we would, by faith, appropriate the same promises for ourselves!

Just as in days of old – perhaps even more so now –there are forces at work in each of our lives to hold us back from God's promise and our potential. The scripture refers to these forces as "yokes" – restrictive bonds used for controlling beasts of burden or slaves. One who is under a "yoke" is not free to follow his dreams. Addictions, afflictions, betrayals, bitterness, critics, crises, debts, divorces, embarrassments, excuses, false friends – and the list of "yokes" that are limiting our progress could go on and on. I think that you get the point. In fact, you could probably add some items to the list. But today is the day for change! This is the appointed time, if we will but embrace it.

In our text, Israel was not being oppressed without a reason. Her sin was the cause of her suffering. Sin had resulted in divine judgment at the hands of hostile foreign powers. While I may not know what your "yoke" is, I do know how it came to be. There are two reasons for "yokes" in our lives: 1. What we have done (our sin and disobedience which have given the enemy an opening to attack); and 2. What we are about to do (our potential in God). Although God may allow us to be tested and tried or even chastened through the "yokes" of the enemy, rest assured that His plan for us is no less than total victory. Get this in your spirit today: You were not designed for defeat or failure, only for success and victory!

Your oppressor is not omnipotent. He has a time limit for what he can do in your life. Hear the Lord saying, "And it shall come to pass in that day, that his burden shall be taken away from off thy shoulder..." It shall be taken away from off your shoulder, not because the enemy volunteered to leave you alone, but because you have the Mighty One intervening on your behalf. It is one thing to carry burdens of purpose and destiny, and another thing entirely to carry burdens of persecution and degradation. Those burdens that have hindered rather than helped your spiritual advancement are about to be removed from off your shoulders:

"...And the yoke from off thy neck..." God promises that what has contained and controlled you will have power over you no longer. In fact, the Lord goes on to say that "...the yoke shall be destroyed because of the anointing." Those things that have restricted, limited and intimidated us in the past will no longer have the capacity even to incite fear in our hearts!

In closing, I want to take a moment to focus on two words in the text. They are the words "destroy" and "anointing."

It is significant to note that the word rendered "destroy" in our text is derived from a root meaning of "to wind tightly (as a rope), to bind." What does this have to do with destroying the yokes in our lives? Well, the common usage is figurative, meaning, "to pervert or destroy, offend, spoil, or corrupt." In other words, God turns the enemy's own tactics against him and the binder becomes the bound. The weapons of the enemy cannot "prosper" against the child of God because God twists and reverses them back on themselves. What was binding you will be rendered ineffective because it is tied in knots!

What is it that will remove the burdens and destroy the yokes from our lives? The text tells us that it is the "anointing." Interestingly the word rendered "anointing" here means "grease," but is also rendered as, "richness, anointing, fat and fruitful." It is clear then, that the deliverance in our lives will come not just as a result of the power of God, but also because of the prosperity of God. One translation says, "the yoke will be broken because you have grown so fat" (Isaiah 10:27 NIV). The image is that of a sturdy, well-fed animal that becomes strong enough to break the yoke!

Can you receive it? Can you believe that God can so bless and empower you that you will throw off and tie up everything that the enemy designed to bind you? The Yoke Destroyer is working even now on your behalf!

TAKE ACTION!

Thoughts for your Journal:
- ➤ What "yokes" do you feel the enemy has placed in your life to contain (hinder) and control you? Are they because of sin or disobedience in your life or because of the promise of God upon your life?
- ➤ How have you been delayed or hindered from achieving your destiny in God? What do you feel the Holy Spirit is instructing you to do about it?

Prayer Focus:
- ➤ Ask the Lord to destroy every yoke that is hindering your progress – spiritual, financial, and otherwise – and the progress of all that concerns you.
- ➤ Pray in Jesus' Name that He will free everyone who is connected to you from any bondage that might hinder your mutual destiny.

Suggested Bible Reading:
- ➤ Proverbs 29
- ➤ Isaiah 10: 20 - 27
- ➤ I John 2

Day Eighteen
Soaring in a Strange Land: Keys to Your Next Promotion

Focus Verses: *"How shall we sing the LORD'S song in a strange land?"* (Psalm 137: 4 KJV)

"Then the king made Daniel a great man, and gave him many great gifts, and made him ruler over the whole province of Babylon, and chief of the governors over the wise men of Babylon." (Daniel 2:48 KJV)

Same site. Same circumstance. Different response. Disparate results. Psalm 137, that plaintive song of the exile, has resonated with beleaguered believers throughout the ages. It's most poignant question, "How shall we sing the LORD'S song in a strange land?" transcends time and place. Anyone who has experienced the bitterness of an enforced stay in an undesirable place or situation knows that a "strange land" need not be miles from where you were born. Anyone who has known love, loss, and longing can respect the psalmist's choice to "hang up his harp" and silence all celebration in tacit testimony to his anguished soul.

If we've lived long enough, we've been where the psalmist was. You may recall that Daniel offers an intriguing alternative to the psalmist's lament. Rather than choosing to "hang it up," Daniel, along with three of his friends, chose to adjust to the new surroundings and rise to undreamed of heights. He chose not only to "sing," but also to soar in a "strange land."

Same site. Both the psalmist and Daniel experienced being in the same place, Babylon, the land of captivity. Babylon, for the exiled people of Judah, was a place where wickedness reigned supreme. It was a place where opportunity seemed restricted. It was a place of alien customs and language – a strange land.

Same circumstance. Both the psalmist and Daniel were captives, exiled from the land of promise. They had both known status and affluence, but now knew what it meant to be less than second-class citizens –nobodies.

Different response. It has been said that the one truly inalienable right we possess is our right to choose how we respond to what happens in our lives. It is this choice, as Daniel deftly demonstrates, that makes all the difference in our destiny. At a time when others were hanging up their harps and silencing their songs, Daniel made another choice. He chose to rise, to soar in the land of oppression.

How did Daniel make such a daring and different decision – the choice to thrive in the very place where others were struggling merely to survive? How did he resolve to soar where others weren't even singing? The answer is both simple and profound – Daniel had a different perspective that caused him to make a different response to his situation. In other words, his attitude determined his altitude.

What was so different about Daniel's outlook? As we read the first two chapters of Daniel, we can infer three striking contrasts between Daniel's viewpoint and that of the sorrowful psalmist.

First, Daniel apparently understood that God had not only allowed his captivity, He had instigated it. Daniel 1: 2 says, "...the Lord gave Jehoiakim king of Judah into his [Nebuchadnezzar's] hand..." Daniel realized that the Lord was behind and in charge of the circumstances in which he found himself. Further, he knew enough about God to know that even in His judgment there is mercy. When we realize that no matter how our current situation may look, our fate is not in the hands of men, we go from hopelessness to hope. Informed by this perspective, we can become open to opportunity, even in our adversity. With Joseph, son of Jacob, we proclaim that although men meant what we have been going through for evil, God meant it for good! (Genesis 50: 20).

Secondly, Daniel realized what most of us miss when we are "going through." He understood that captivity was proof of the favor on his life. King Nebuchadnezzar gave orders that only certain of the children of Israel were to be brought back to Babylon – young men from the royal line with no physical defect, handsome, showing aptitude for every kind of learning, well-informed and qualified to serve in the king's palace (Daniel 1:3-4). Daniel was smart enough to discern from the context clues that he was taken captive because he was among the select few with enough favor to be chosen. How different our perspective might be if we realized that – that we have been picked out to be picked on; that what we go through is because of God's hand upon us and His destiny within us. How often have I with tears in my eyes said, "Why me?" Daniel was savvy enough to say, "Why not me?" If only we could remember that whatever difficulties God's favor brings us to, He is more than able to bring us through!

Thirdly, I think that Daniel understood the history of his people well enough to remember that some of the greatest promises and promotions come not in the familiar surroundings of the believer's home, but in the foreign territories outside his or her comfort zone. Daniel may have remembered that when God wanted to bless Abraham, He took him from his father's house and kindred. Perhaps he recalled that it was in the latently hostile environment of his Uncle Laban's house, that God began to enlarge Jacob. No doubt he took into account that it was in Egypt that Joseph became great, and that it was from exile that Moses was launched into his destiny. Have you found yourself in a "strange land," a place far, far from your comfort zone? Perhaps it is the prelude for your next promotion.

TAKE ACTION!

Thoughts for your Journal:
- ➢ Do you see your attitude as being more like that of Daniel who soared in the "strange land," or more like the psalmist of Psalm 137, who hung up his harp?
- ➢ What have been the results of your perspective in the past?
- ➢ What adjustments, if any, are necessary for your next promotion?

Prayer Focus:
- ➢ Ask God to help you to remember that no matter how things may look around you, your times are in His hands, and that He has not designed you to be defeated, but to walk in victory.

Suggested Bible Reading:
- ➢ Proverbs 13
- ➢ Isaiah 40
- ➢ Daniel 1 & 2

Day Nineteen
Soaring in a Strange Land- Pt. II

Focus Verses: *"How shall we sing the LORD'S song in a strange land?"* (Psalm 137: 4 KJV)

"Then the king made Daniel a great man, and gave him many great gifts, and made him ruler over the whole province of Babylon, and chief of the governors over the wise men of Babylon." (Daniel 2:48 KJV)

Yesterday, we discussed how Daniel, a contemporary of the psalmist of Psalm 137, chose an intriguing alternative to the psalmist's approach. Rather than choosing to "hang it up" – as the Psalmist did – Daniel chose to acclimate to his new surroundings and rise to undreamed of heights. He chose not only to "sing," but also to soar in a "strange land." As thinking people, we can't help but wonder whether God is behind what we are going through? How do we know if what we are experiencing is because of God's favor, and not just man's failure? On a more personal note, how can I know if my current situation is indeed the prelude for my next promotion and not just the first sad notes of my "swan song"? Good questions, but not questions that I can presume to answer for you. Only you can say whether any of these lessons from Daniel's life resonate with what God is saying and doing within you.

Have you found yourself "exiled" from the land of your promises – a stranger in a "strange land"? Have you recently experienced a sudden and even painful change in status? Do you have the faith to believe that even in what you're going through, God is still in charge of your life, working out His good purposes even though you can't understand what He is doing and why? Then perhaps this is for you. Quite honestly, even if your current situation is the result of failure and not favor, following Daniel's example will transform your "strange land" into a land of promise and position you for your next promotion! Let's consider then, what other lessons Daniel has to offer about how to "soar in a strange land."

The fourth key that we can take from Daniel's story is, Promotion comes to those who refuse to allow where they are to dictate who they are. Daniel was a captive in a foreign country, renamed by his oppressor, and immersed in an alien culture. It would have been easy to get along by going along, to say, "When in Babylon, do as the Babylonians..." But Daniel purposed that he would not lose his identity – that he would not "defile himself" with the king's food (Daniel 1: 16). He chose even in captivity to embrace a lifestyle of consecration before God. A courageous decision made at great personal risk and with no little personal discomfort. Daniel refused to be stripped of his God-given uniqueness. We might do well to remember in our age of situational ethics and spirituality without sacrifice that true worth is achieved not by fitting in with the crowd, but by being willing to be distinguished from them!

The fifth key – Promotion awaits the Praiser. I'm almost embarrassed to write this because it seems so simple that it is almost clichéd. But the Lord won't allow me to pass over this truth. In Daniel chapter two, we see that Daniel was a praiser, whether in private or in public. He gave God glory not just in the presence of "home boys" from Judah, but in the throne room of the enemy king (Daniel 2: 20-23, 28). Later, in chapter six, we see even after many years that Daniel is still not embarrassed about his prayer and praise life, even when under threat of execution. Daniel was an outstanding candidate for promotion because he knew where promotion really comes from, and made it his business to stay in favor with the One who was able to elevate him even in exile. How often I have withheld praise waiting for a more "appropriate time." The fact is that there is never an inappropriate time to give God glory. Even if I can't break out in a dance or turn cartwheels, when afforded the opportunity, I can always give credit to the One who has made all good things possible!

Finally, we can learn from Daniel's elevation in an unlikely setting that, Promotion comes to those who can discern and deliver the lost dreams of others. There is probably an entire book in this one statement. One prominent local church leadership consultant and author, Dr. Samuel Chand refers to himself as a "Dream Releaser." I like that. The thing that set Daniel apart from all the other wise men in the kingdom was that he was able to discern and release a "lost dream." King Nebuchadnezzar knew that he had a dream but didn't know what it was (Daniel 2: 2- 5). He needed someone to retrieve the dream from his lost memory files and then interpret it for him.

Daniel distinguished himself by being able (through God) to discover the lost dream. We live in a world of lost dreams. We are surrounded by people great and small who know that there is a dream in them, but have no clue as to what it is or what it might mean. True greatness is reserved for those who can find and release lost dreams! People who can take the focus off themselves long enough to look into the eyes of men and the heart of God can bring divine revelation from heaven to earth. Is it possible that unless and until I assist someone else with their dream, as did Daniel, my own dream will remain dormant and unfulfilled?

Same site. Same circumstance. Different response. Disparate results. Two men: one overcome with grief and despondency – the other, propelled into destiny. We may not be able to choose where we are in life. We may not be able to choose our circumstances. We can always choose our response and that makes all the difference!

TAKE ACTION!

Thoughts for your Journal:
- ➢ In what ways have your circumstances dictated how you perceive yourself?
- ➢ As you look at your current circumstances, is there anyone whose dreams God may have assigned you to reveal and release as a key to your next promotion?

Prayer Focus:
- ➢ Pray that God will help you to live life on purpose – His purposes not your own. Ask Him to help you to see beyond your own experiences and feelings so that you may touch and bless those He has assigned you to impact for Him.

Suggested Bible Reading:
- ➢ Proverbs 4
- ➢ Psalm 139
- ➢ Daniel1&2

Day Twenty
Beginning At The End!

Focus Verse: *"Brethren, I count not myself to have apprehended: but this one thing I do, forgetting those things which are behind, and reaching forth unto those which are before, I press toward the mark for the prize of the high calling of God in Christ Jesus."* (Philippians 3: 13 KJV)

Every new beginning starts with an ending. Some doors only open after all other doors have closed. We're poised, you and I, on the brink of a new and exciting future, but there are some conclusions – doors that must be closed – before we can cross into it. Closure comes in two parts – our part and God's part. Today, I want us to look at the part we can play in preparing for our new beginning. I came across the following words years ago and copied them down although I'm embarrassed to admit, I don't know who wrote them:

"If you don't like your present life situation, you don't have to stay attached to it. Just put a period at the end of your current life experiences and bring this chapter of your life to a close. Get ready to write a more exciting chapter tomorrow. All you have to do is employ that wonderful punctuation mark that signifies completion. A period indicates the old is finished. A period signifies the new can now begin. It is easy to stay attached to something even though it no longer benefits you. The path of dogged but unrewarding effort is well traveled. You can easily fall into a rut and stay there. After all, doing nothing is often the path of least resistance. It is also the path of passivity and death. It takes courage to bring the old to a close. It takes imagination and effort to create the new."

Have you noticed that it is almost impossible to really reach toward the future while tied down to the past? In order for some things to come in your life, some other things have to end. Decide today, right now to let go of what is holding you back. Here are some things that you might want to consider letting go of:

> **The Past** - good or bad, the fact remains that it is over. People who are obsessed with the past are unable to respond appropriately to what is happening in the present; they're too busy revisiting and trying to revise what happened then.

> Constantly reliving past accomplishments can soon become a hindrance to future conquests. Decide to let go of the past with its pain and pleasure. Your greatest days lie just ahead. Go for them!

> **Guilt** - a lot of people don't realize that there is a difference between guilt and remorse. Guilt is a totally useless emotion that only makes you feel bad and tempts you to more bad choices in the attempt to drive it away. Remorse is akin to biblical repentance. It leads

to a resolve not to repeat the same errors and sins again. How to deal with guilt? Confess your sins; bite the bullet, make apologies and restitution where possible; resolve to go in another direction.

➢ **Resentment** - Nothing ruins your happiness, your future relationships or your decision-making power as easily as resentment. Has someone hurt you? Let it go and focus on what you can do to make things right, or simply distance yourself, if need be. By all means refuse to be a prisoner of resentment and bitterness. Resentment is like guilt; it's all about you and your own "righteousness." It tricks you into a never-ending cycle of pain as you constantly replay the past. You don't need a continual, constant reminder of how much it hurt.

➢ **Revenge** - The old saying goes, "revenge is a dish best served up cold." The truth of the matter is that revenge is a dish best thrown away. Was nursing an obsession with getting-even a part of your original dream for your life? Did you sit and daydream years ago about a "golden" future filled with revenge? It has been said that revenge only reinforces the original hurt, creates another enemy, warps your judgment, and takes your focus away from where it should be – on fulfilling your destiny in God! Revenge will lead into a cycle of actions and behaviors that will ultimately cause you to hate yourself as much as you hate the one who hurt you. Decide now. Let it go!

I could go on and on, but the point here is that each of us needs to make our own the list of what we need to let go of. What do you see missing from this list as pertains to your life?

Bad habits? Sins of the flesh or spirit? Laziness? Prayerlessness? A covetous spirit (the unwillingness to give to God or others)? Pride? Self-righteousness?

Listen to God today. Really listen. He is waiting to usher you into a wonderful time of "newness" in Him as you bring conclusion to your past.

"You see that is true life. Life is found in death. It is found in dying to self and living to Jesus Christ. In recognizing that the very meaning of life was shown to us through the life of Jesus and saying, 'God, that is how I want it. Please live your life in me.' The question before us now is, do we want to live life as God intended, or do we want to continue on our own, to search for it in the futile corners, in the tidbits that the world would throw us? .... Contemplate, and don't be afraid to come to conclusion and closure and say that from this time on I want to live life as God intended it." – Lee R. Lescano

TAKE ACTION!

Thoughts for your Journal:
- ➤ Make your own list of things that by God's help, you want to bring to a conclusion in your life.
- ➤ Reflect on which relationships need to be revisited in order to bring closure and conclusion. Do you need to make things right with anyone? Are there some relationships that are not conducive to your walk with God that need to be ended (I am not speaking here of ending a marriage, or getting rid of your children)?

Prayer Focus:
- ➤ Pray for the light of the Holy Spirit to reveal the things that you need to conclude or let go of, in order for this to be your greatest year.

Suggested Bible Reading:
- ➤ II Samuel 12: 13 - 24
- ➤ Philippians 3

Day Twenty-One
Beginning At The End – Pt. II

Focus Verse: *"Then said I, Woe is me! for I am undone; because I am a man of unclean lips, and I dwell in the midst of a people of unclean lips: for mine eyes have seen the King, the LORD of hosts."* (Isaiah 6:5 NKJV)

Yesterday we looked at essential endings, from a human point of view. Our focus was on the part that we must play in making necessary closure in our lives. Today let's focus on God's part. In his life-changing encounter with the Almighty, the Prophet Isaiah lamented his unworthiness to do the work of God. Isaiah's acknowledgement of so long ago is our predicament today. Like him, we have a vision of God's greatness and of what He wants to do in our lives, but we are hindered by the limitations of our fleshly flaws. There are some issues in our lives that only God can resolve. The good news is that God stands ready and able to give victory in those areas where we are powerless!

"Then flew one of the seraphims unto me, having a live coal in his hand, which he had taken with the tongs from off the altar. And he

laid it upon my mouth, and said, Lo, this hath touched thy lips; and thine iniquity is taken away, and thy sin is purged." (Isaiah 6: 6, 7 NKJV)

Yesterday we discussed "letting go" of hindrances. But what are we to do about the hindrances that won't "let go" of us? These are issues that we need to bring to our loving Father. Here are some areas where His deliverance might be warranted:

➤ **Bands of wickedness** - sinful, destructive behaviors and patterns that have taken such a hold on our spirit and soul that only God can break them. These could include addictive behaviors, ungodly soul ties, and persistent but seemingly inconsequential areas of sin in our lives. God wants to set us free as a result of this journey in fasting and prayer!

➤ **Wounds of Soul and Spirit** - God alone is able to heal those wounds that go down so deep that you can't even really talk about them. He awaits our invitation...but when He does the work, you must make the conscious choice not to go and pick it up again.

➤ **The Spirit of Debt and Poverty** - Yes, poverty and debt can be spiritual. God is able to show us how these destructive spirits gained entrance into our lives, and bring deliverance. Deliverance in this area, as in every other area, requires repentance.

➤ **Spirits of Infirmity** - Has it occurred to you that some of the physical maladies with which we suffer might be spiritual in origin? If it seems that no sooner than you get over one physical challenge, another is waiting, it might be that you need God to deliver you from the spirit of infirmity.

You can probably add to this list. But the point is that God wants to do some things in our lives that we can't do for ourselves. Will you trust Him? Will you honestly lay your secret hindrances before Him?

I must be honest with you. Deliverance may not be painless. I wonder if Isaiah was scarred by the live coal from the altar that touched his lips. I know that Jacob walked with a permanent limp from his encounter with the Lord at Peniel. But the fact is that both men were permanently changed, never again to be as they were. If God, for example, removes an unwholesome soul-tie from your life, it might hurt. But the power that will be released in your life will be worth the pain. Let God do what He wants to do. Let Him deliver you. You are created for victory. If you are living beneath your purpose, you are probably living in pain anyway. Birth is accompanied by pain, but after the child arrives, the joy outweighs the pain. What God wants to "birth" in us will bring a joy that outweighs any temporary discomfort our deliverance might entail.

I am reminded the chorus of an old hymn that I used to hear my parents sing:

"His power can make you what you ought to be;
His blood can cleanse your soul and make you free;
His love will fill your heart and you will see;
Twas best for Him to have His way with thee".

TAKE ACTION!

Thoughts for your Journal:
> ➤ Reflect and list those areas of conclusion that only God can bring in your life.
> ➤ What areas are going to require repentance, confession or restitution on your part? Resolve now not to hide, justify or whitewash your sins.

Prayer Focus:
> ➤ Pray for the light of the Holy Spirit to reveal the things that you need His help to bring conclusion to, especially areas in which, up until now, you have been in denial, or have been trying to handle in your human power.

Suggested Bible Reading:
> ➤ Isaiah 58
> ➤ Romans 6 – 8

Fuel Stop
Stepping Toward Your Goals!

"The secret of getting ahead is getting started. The secret of getting started is breaking your complex, overwhelming tasks into manageable tasks, and then starting on the first one."
-Mark Twain

As important as clear, specific, measurable, dated goals are, they will remain lifeless and irrelevant without Action Plans to ensure their fulfillment. Each major goal on your list deserves an Action Plan – a list of the successive steps or actions that must be taken to achieve that goal, along with target dates for their completion. Action Plans will enable you to treat each goal as the single project that it is. Breaking down a large goal into smaller tasks – to be accomplished one at a time – is how a big goal gets achieved.

Once you have determined what you really want and created definite, written goals, you must figure out the successive steps that will be needed to accomplish each goal. For many of your goals, this will be easy to do. But there will be some goals that you will have no idea how to achieve. What to do? There are several ways to figure out what steps will need to be taken to complete any goal. Here are two:

1. Seek out people who have already done what you are attempting to do and ask what steps they took. Learn from their experiences, not only the necessary steps, but also the pitfalls to avoid. If you don't personally know anyone who has done what you are trying to do, you may be able to achieve the same objective by

purchasing a book or a manual that outlines the process. Remember, it is fine not to know how to do a thing. There is nothing wrong with asking for guidance and advice. And if approached correctly (not as one looking for a handout), many people are flattered by being sought out for their life experiences and wisdom.

2. Another way to ascertain the steps needed for your Action Plan is to start from the end and look backward. Imagine that you are in the future and that the goal has been successfully achieved. What did you have to do to get it done. What was the last step in the process of completion of the goal? What was the thing that had to be done before that?

Keep going back a step at a time until you arrive at the first thing you would've done toward the completion of the goal.

Action Plan Challenge

Make the time between today and tomorrow to create Action Plans for every major goal on your goal list. Assign a sheet of paper to each individual goal, create a number list for the action steps from top to bottom. Make sure that there is space on the page for a start date and a completion date for every objective/step on the list. Notice that as your mind begins working on establishing your objectives for each goal, you may find that you are constantly adding to your list. Each question that needs an answer becomes an objective. Each action you must take becomes an objective. Each resource that you must gather becomes an objective. But when taken together all of these objectives or action steps are a dynamic, step-by-step Action Plan!

Remember, breaking down goals into written objectives is one of the most important, overlooked secrets of Winners. Systematically completing individual objectives will always result in the completion of goals.

This, in turn, will double both your power to achieve and your personal effectiveness!

Day Twenty-Two
Tap Into Your Power!

Focus Verses: *"He giveth power to the faint; and to them that have no might He increaseth strength. Even the youths shall faint and be weary, and the young men shall utterly fall: But they that wait upon the Lord shall renew their strength; they shall mount up with wings as eagles; they shall run and not be weary; and they shall walk, and not faint."* (Isaiah 40: 29-31 KJV)

From the cradle to the grave, human life might be described as one long power struggle. Before we can speak, walk or even feed ourselves, we are tiny soldiers battling to assert power over the world around us through the only media available to us – our smiles, screams and tears. As we grow, we become more skilled at games of manipulation and control. We learn early that he who loves least often wields the most power and thus, in our quest for domination, we become adept at emotionally engaging and disengaging. We travel through life attempting to control others so that, if for no other reason, we may feel that we have more control over our own lives. As we mature, we come to see the acquisition of power as a means to get things done, the ability to accomplish our destiny. We come to realize that our greatest struggle in life is for the power of self-determination.

When we are saved and bow to the Lordship of Jesus Christ, we surrender our desire for self-determination as we allow Him to chart our course. But more than ever we find that we still need power. We need the power of self-discipline. We need power over the enemy who constantly seeks to attack us and hinder our journey. We need what the old saints called "walk-right, talk-right and do-right power!" We also long to know that we have power with our God, that when we cry He will indeed answer and come to our aid.

Enough. I can no longer presume to speak for you. Allow me to speak for myself and confess that in more than 40 years of walking with God, I have prayed often with tears and great passion for more of His power – the ability to strive, survive, and succeed in life. Even as I type these words, I feel that longing stirring in my breast – I need power not to dominate others, but to discipline myself; not to bend the world to my will, but to bend myself to the will of God; not to take from anyone, but to be able to give out freely to all, that which the Lord has deposited in me. I need power to function as a child of God in this wicked world. I need power not to give up the fight short of total victory – power to press the battle to the gate – power not to faint.

During a season of fasting and prayer, I stumbled on a key to accessing divine power, a key that was hidden in plain view. Isaiah gives us that key to spiritual power in our focus verses: *"He giveth power to the faint...they that wait upon the Lord shall renew their strength..."* Like you, I have read these verses a thousand times. But it was only in a prolonged time of prayer that my eyes were opened to the fact that the prophet wasn't speaking figuratively, but literally, when he spoke about waiting on the Lord, *"They that wait upon the Lord shall renew their strength..."*

Waiting is a lost art in prayer. It may be the most effective part of our prayer life, and yet it is the part most of us overlook. Most Christians, even those who pray for hours, come before the Lord, say their piece, make petitions, and even cry out their supplications; only to then get up and go about their business, thinking that they are waiting on the Lord to answer our prayers. Isaiah shares with those who will hear him, the overlooked key – that waiting on the Lord is not something we do between prayer meetings; it is a vital part of our time in prayer. In fact, it may be the most effective part of prayer.

Waiting on the Lord might be defined as patiently lingering in His presence. When is the last time that, after praying, you just quietly stayed in His presence for no other reason than simply that you desired to be with Him? To wait on the Lord is to linger with Him, whether He speaks or not; it is to linger with Him whether anything dramatic happens or not. The fact of matter is that God wants us to love Him enough just to want to "hang out" with Him. Isn't that what we do with anyone else we truly love?

When we wait on the Lord, when we stay with Him just because we long for His presence more than His presents, something happens. He may not say much. We may not see anything. But strangely, when we get up from our time of waiting on God we don't leave empty. We leave with newfound power. We leave from our time of waiting on the Lord with supernatural strength we didn't have before. When we wait upon the Lord, we arise empowered and recharged with the ability to accomplish more than we were able to do before. No wonder Jesus instructed His disciples to go to

Jerusalem and wait there until endued with power from on high (Luke 24:49). Those early saints waited on the Lord, not by going back to Jerusalem and carrying on business as usual, but by staying continually in prayer and praise. They waited on the Lord, and when the day of Pentecost had fully come, they were endued with the promised power!

Are you tired? Weary in the battle of life? In need of more power to accomplish God's purpose for your life? Determine today to tap into the power that is waiting for you, by waiting on the Lord!

TAKE ACTION!

Thoughts for your Journal:
> ➤ Can you point to a time when you lingered in the presence of the Lord after praying? What were the results of your waiting?
> ➤ In what areas of your life do you currently need more power from the Lord?

Prayer Focus:
> ➤ Pray for a praying spirit, and the ability and willingness to linger in His presence until, you, like the apostles of old, are endued with supernatural power.

Suggested Bible Reading:
> ➤ Isaiah 40
> ➤ Acts 1 – 2

Day Twenty-Three
Ant-ology 101:
Confessions of a Grasshopper

Focus Verse: *"Go to the ant, thou sluggard; consider her ways and be wise..."* (Proverbs 6: 6 KJV)

I have to tell you that it was strangely difficult for me to write this devotional thought. I just couldn't find any enthusiasm about going to "ant school." Ants. Boring creatures, really – working, working, working all the time. Ants. I imagine them marching in martial formation, chanting some mindless mantra as they embark on a never-ending list of tedious tasks. Ants. Do they ever stop to play? To sing or dance? To marvel at a work of art or wonder at the grandeur of a golden sunset? Grasshoppers do. It pains me to admit it, but there is something in me that relates to the grasshopper – happy and carefree, unpredictable, with music and dance built in to his very system. Ants may get it done, but grasshoppers have more fun.

I love the way Rev. R. D. Mangold, envisions an "ant congregation" in his blog, "Go to the Ant" (*Apostolic Flashpoint*, October 12, 2007):

"In my wild imagination, I envision a tiny little ant, in his Sunday-best, stepping to the pulpit, and tapping the microphone to ensure it's operational. Shrill feedback reverberates through the congregation. After a rousing chorus of, "Ant He walks with me, ant He talks with me," Rever-ant clears his nervous throat, and leafs through his well-rehearsed manuscript. With antennae at the ready, he rears back and belts out the proverbial gospel of, "work while it is day, for the night cometh when no ant can work!" To which this copious colony returns a resounding, "Amen!""

I can imagine that before the sermon is over, the "rever-ant" probably touches on "sluggards," casting a pointed glance in the direction of the grasshoppers in the congregation. Ouch. I may be a grasshopper, but I never signed on to be called a "sluggard." Aren't "sluggards" sleepy, slow-moving, and lazy? That's not me. We grasshoppers are quick, agile and active. But wait, what is this I hear the "rever-ant" saying? The word "sluggard" doesn't necessarily mean sleepy or slow-moving, rather, it means, "a self-indulgent person who spends time avoiding work or other useful activity." Now, that is beginning to sound uncomfortably close to home. I can hear one of my grasshopper brethren saying, "I resemble that remark."

The primary difference between the proverbial grasshopper and the ant, is not the in the degree of activity, but in the productivity of the activity. In other words, grasshoppers are busy, but not productive – often proudly so.

In *Three Men in a Boat*, English author Jerome K. Jerome, described the grasshopper's work ethic, "I like work; it fascinates me. I can sit and look at it for hours. I love to keep it by me: the idea of getting rid of it nearly breaks my heart."

What can a creature with a microscopic brain teach us about life and work anyway? Well, as it turns out, it can teach us a lot. Stephen Vincent Benét said, "The ant finds kingdoms in a foot of ground." We learn from the ant, for example, that each of us has our own job to do in our own sphere – things that we cannot, or at least should not, hand over to anyone else. The ant also teaches us that rest is a reward to be enjoyed only after the work is done. Here is the kicker: although grasshoppers are multiple times the size of ants, there is also a big difference in their life expectancy. Grasshoppers once hatched from the egg, never survive through the winter. Worker ants can survive up to three years (not to mention the queen that survives up to 30 years) – an amazingly long time for such small creatures. What else can we learn from the ant? Check out the book of Proverbs. In the meantime, does anyone know where I can turn in my "grasshopper card?"

TAKE ACTION!

Thoughts for your Journal:
> ➢ Are you an "ant" or a "grasshopper"? Why did you answer as you did?
> ➢ If you admitted to being a "grasshopper", list the important things that you have avoided doing because of "unproductive busy-ness." Put action dates on each item.

Prayer Focus:
> ➢ Ask the Lord to show you any "grasshopper" tendencies in your character that might be hindering your spiritual progress.

Suggested Bible Reading:
> ➢ Proverbs 6
> ➢ Genesis 13 - 15
> ➢ Matthew 5

Day Twenty-Four
To Death?

Focus Verse: *"Do not fear any of those things which you are about to suffer.... Be faithful unto death, and I will give you the crown of life."* (Revelation 2: 10 NKJV)

When I was growing up, it was fairly common to hear people say something like this: *"I love you to death."* It was a figurative way of expressing deep and abiding affection – a way of saying, *"I really mean it, when I tell you that I love you."* Like many popular expressions that fall into disuse, you don't hear those words as much anymore. Maybe that is a reflection of the world in which we live. People love, but not quite that deeply. Few people love anything or anybody "to death" anymore. In fact, most marriages are entered into with no notion of permanence. I wouldn't be surprised if in the next few years the words, "'Til Death Do Us Part" are dropped from the wedding vows entirely. Loyalty has become a lost concept. Most people nowadays go through a parade of jobs, homes, cars, and relationships in a lifetime. We have become so "consumer minded" that we evaluate everything we are involved in strictly in terms of, "What is in it for me?" And if we determine that the return doesn't justify the investment, we are "out of there" in a flash – whether it is a job or a relationship. We tend to evaluate people on the basis of what they "bring to the table." We even measure our own personal worth in the "currency" of our talent and ability, more than our loyalty or stability.

Unfortunately, this mentality often bleeds over into our relationship with God. We have an attitude that says, "Wherever God guides, He provides," which sounds good to our modern ears. The flip side of the statement is, "If His isn't providing, He must not have been guiding." This in turn gives us an out when things become difficult in our lives of serving Him.

But is that statement really true? The life and testimony of St. Paul, who writes about suffering lack and hardship in the service of the Lord, would cause me to doubt the truth of that expression. Just a look at Paul's life and struggle seems to indicate that sometimes it is possible to be in the will of God and yet suffer hunger and deprivation, even shipwreck. The witness of the martyrs in Hebrews 11 also seems to undermine that thought. For the record shows that these were people, some of whom were destitute and even naked, but perfectly in the will of God..."to death."

Yes, where the Lord guides, He does provide, but not always in the ways in which we expect or even desire Him to provide. He refuses to be locked into a strictly transactional relationship in which we say, "Here is what I am bringing to the table. Lord, by the way, what have You done for me lately?" Believe it or not, God is not impressed by talent, intelligence or anything else you or I have to offer Him. He is impressed by one all important thing – our loyalty, our decision to be faithful to Him and to His cause no matter what, even when it doesn't seem to be paying off in rich dividends. He is looking for folks who love Him..."to death."

And that brings me to the word that I have felt led to share with you today. I seem to hear the Word of the Lord whispering in my ear, "Be faithful unto death, and I will give you a crown of life." We may not all be able to sing or preach or touch the masses. We may not all be "five-talent" people. We may not all be in the public limelight. But we can all choose to prove our love for Him by being faithful. That means placing His agenda above our wishes, putting His purposes at the top of our priorities, and placing His cause above our own comfort. If you are still seeking to save your life or to place the American Dream above the Vision of the Cross, it means that you have missed the point.

Commitment isn't real unless it cuts into your flesh. It isn't real unless it results in sacrifices of time, talent, and treasure that seem to be imprudent and outrageous to casual spectators. I hear the Lord speaking in my spirit that only those who are willing to make that kind of commitment will experience the Supernatural in their lives. The question we must ask ourselves is this: "Do I really love God? Do I love Him with all my heart? Do I love Him to Death?" If I do, there is only one way to prove it. I must take up my cross and be "faithful unto death."

He loved us..."To Death."

TAKE ACTION!

Thoughts for your Journal:
- ➤ On a scale of 1-10 (and this is totally between you and God) rate your commitment level to God? What is the basis of your score?
- ➤ Reflection: in what areas do you most need to step up your commitment to God?

Prayer Focus:
- ➤ Pray for the Holy Spirit to give you a fresh revelation of the kind of commitment that God is calling for in your life.
- ➤ Pray for a corporate revelation among Christians, locally, nationally & internationally of the level of commitment God is calling for.

Suggested Bible Reading:
- ➤ Luke 9: 23-27
- ➤ Acts 20: 17-31
- ➤ 2 Corinthians 11: 16-33
- ➤ Hebrews 11

Day Twenty-Five
Using Your Greatest Ability!

Focus Verses: *"When Jesus saw him lying there and learned that he had been in this condition for a long time, he asked him, "Do you want to get well?"* (John 5: 6 NIV)

"I can do all things through Christ who strengthens me." (Philippians 4: 13 NIV)

No matter how great last year may have been for you, if you are like most people I know – myself included – you are not fully satisfied with where you are in life. Today is about self-empowerment. It is about making a promise to yourself that starting this moment, you will no longer be the victim of circumstances outside your control. Starting this moment, the wait is over. We will no longer wait for the stars to align in our favor – or for Iyanla Vanzant, "Dr. Phil" McGraw, Oprah Winfrey or anyone else to "fix" our lives. We are far more powerful – you and I – than we ever previously imagined! Here is something that I've learned:

If you want to change your life for the better, you must begin by tapping into your greatest ability. It is that ability which each of us shares – the ability to choose our response to whatever circumstances life hands us. This is big. Most of us have been conditioned to blame someone or something outside ourselves for those aspects of our lives that we don't like. We have allowed ourselves to become stymied by the things that have happened...or not happened in our lives, to the point of becoming stuck. Well, today would be a great day to get "un-stuck!" You have the power to change your life, because no matter what is going on right now you have the ability to choose your response. That's your greatest ability. You have "Response-ability" for everything that happens in your life.

Taking "response-ability" for your life means choosing to give up all excuses. George Washington Carver said, "Ninety-nine percent of all failures come from people who have a habit of making excuses." You have the power, through God, to make things different, to produce the desired results. You've always had it. Truly you *can "do all things through Christ"* (Philippians 4:13). But for whatever reason – ignorance, fear, lack of faith, a need to be "right" –most of us have failed to exercise our power of response. Instead, like the lame man who had waited for years for the right circumstances for his healing (John 5), we have chosen to make excuses as to why we remain in the state we are in. Today, that ends!

One reason why we fail to use the power of "response-ability" is that we have mistaken events in our lives for outcomes. There is a difference, you know. The events of our lives are the things that happen to us over which we have little or no control. We often mistake them for outcomes because the impact seems to be so final and far-reaching. Being sexually molested or being raised by a drunken parent or growing up in a broken home are just a few examples of events that happen in many of our lives; events with such pervasive impact that we are tempted to feel that they are final outcomes.

Many feel that their hopes and dreams in life have been shattered by such painful events. How many of us have heard people say things that express this underlying sentiment: "I am failing in life because of certain events that happened in my past." However, upon closer inspection, we find other people who have experienced similar devastation, but have gone on to create productive, successful, fulfilling lives. If the event – pain from our past, for example – is the conclusive, deciding variable, then everyone who has had that experience would have the same, identical result in their life. But clearly that's not the case. It is the individual response to each event that determines the final outcome.

What I am really saying is that the final chapter of your story has not been written. No matter what has happened up until now, you still have the opportunity to write the "next chapter" by the response you choose to live out! Yes, there may be economic recession, but you can decide not to participate. Yes, there may be a great decline in national church attendance church and participation, but you can decide to draw closer to God.

The unpleasant truth is that most of what we are experiencing today is the result of choices we made in the past. But the good news is that what we experience tomorrow will be the result of the choices we make today! What kinds of choices are you making today?

Why not choose not only to give up the luxury of making excuses, but also to let go of blaming and complaining? Whenever you blame another, you surrender your rightful power over to them. It has been said that all blame is a waste of time. No matter how much fault you find with another, and regardless of how much you blame him, it will not change you." Neither will it change your current circumstances. It's a simple choice, really. You can play the victim or you can walk in victory – but you can't do both! Similarly, complaining is not only a waste of time, it saps away positive energy and initiative. Most of the circumstances people complain about are, by their very nature things that they could change, if only they would take the risk necessary to create a better situation.

In closing, let me just say that the moment you begin to change your responses, your life will begin to get better! Instead of complaining and blaming, try making requests and taking action that will achieve a desirable outcome. You'll love the results! Begin right this moment to tap into your greatest ability, your "response-ability," and create a better life! Now, that's change you can believe in!

TAKE ACTION!

Thoughts for your Journal:
- ➢ Think of and write down any "events" (things that happened to you) in your life that you mistook for final "outcomes"? What response might have been made that might have changed the outcome that you experienced? Are there any current "outcomes" that can be improved by modifying past responses that have you have made?
- ➢ List people or circumstances to which you have surrendered your rightful power by making them responsible for your outcomes. In what ways can you take back your power by choosing a different response?

Prayer Focus:
- ➢ Ask God to forgive you for those times when you have chosen to make excuses or cast blame, rather than make progress in your life.
- ➢ Pray for wisdom to discern the difference between "events" and "outcomes," and for the strength to always choose to take responsibility for your actions and responses.

Suggested Bible Reading:
- ➢ John 5: 1-9
- ➢ Romans 12
- ➢ Philippians 4: 8-13
- ➢ I Thessalonians 5: 15-23

Day Twenty-Six
Look Where You're Going!

Focus Verse: *"So we fix our eyes not on what is seen, but on what is unseen, since what is seen is temporary, but what is unseen is eternal."* (2 Corinthians 4: 18)

It's been over 30 years ago now, but I still remember my father teaching me how to drive. I laugh now, but it wasn't so funny back then. What stands out most in my memory was Dad's fussing. Usually calm and self-controlled, Dad found something about my driving that provoked him to distraction. Upset by my inattentiveness behind the wheel, he would begin to vent, addressing his commentary primarily to my mother who was sitting in the back seat. "Billie," he'd say (using her nickname), "this boy's not driving the car, he's aiming it!" Then he'd turn to me and say, "Steer the car, Son! Don't just aim it and look away! You've got to focus your eyes on where you want the car to go, because wherever you turn your focus is where this car is going to go!" Of course, the more he fussed, the more nervous I became and the more difficult it was to concentrate on getting it right. I still remember that lesson: you've got to LOOK where you want to GO.

This summarizes a major key to personal transformation: If we want our lives to be better we must turn our vision in the direction that we wish to go. Biblical wisdom warns us, *"Where there is no vision, the people perish"* (Prov. 29:18). The most literal translation of that verse of scripture is that without a vision people are left naked. In other words, without a vision we are left to go about "unclothed" for victorious living!

We've all heard the rhetorical question, "If you don't know where you're going, how will you know when you get there?" What is your life vision? Arriving at the life of your dreams begins by asking yourself two questions:

1. Why am I here? (What is your life purpose on this earth?)

2. What will my life look like, if I succeed in fulfilling my purpose? (What is your vision?)

Both are questions you must answer for yourself – questions that take some prayer and thought. Here are some questions that might assist you in identifying and articulating your life purpose:

- ➤ What do you love to do – so much so that you would do it if money weren't an issue?
- ➤ What comes easily to you that others find difficult?
- ➤ What things are you most passionate about?

When you discover and align your life activities around your purposes, the people, resources and opportunities that you need will begin to flow toward you.

Once you've identified your purpose, you will be ready to articulate your vision – a clear mental picture of your desired future. Actor and author, Ben Stein said, "The indispensable first step to getting the things you want out of life is this:

decide what you want." What do you see yourself accomplishing, acquiring and experiencing in life? Open your journal right now and begin to write a vision of your preferred future. What does a well-lived life – your well-lived and purposeful life – look like to you? As you prayerfully begin picturing your ideal life, you may want to consider some of the following vision categories:

> Your ideal financial/material life – what do you envision as your annual income? What does your cash flow look like? How much do you have in savings and investments? What does your home look like? What kind of car do you drive?

> Your ideal job/vocation – where do you work? What do you do? With whom do you work? Who are your clients or customers? Do you own the business?

> Your recreational life – What do you do with family and friends in your free time? What kinds of vacations do you take? What do you do for fun?

> Your relationships – What do your family relationships look like? If you're married, is it a loving marriage? Do you have children? What kind of relationships do you have with them? Who are your friends? What do your friendships feel like? Are they nurturing and encouraging? Do they empower you to become better? What kinds of things do you do with your family and close friends?

> Your physical health and image – Are you free of disease? To what age will you live? Are you full of vitality? Are you at your ideal weight? Are you flexible and strong? Do you exercise, eat a healthy diet and drink lots of water?

> ➤ Your personal growth – Do you see yourself going back to school, pursuing an advanced degree; participating in workshops, attending training sessions or seeking therapy for some past hurts? Are you growing intellectually and emotionally? Do you desire to learn an instrument or how to write a book? Do you see yourself traveling?

> ➤ Your spiritual growth – Are you a person of consistent prayer and study of the Scriptures? Do you share your witness on a consistent basis? Are you active and supportive in a local church? Do you support or actually participate in global missions? How many people will be in heaven because of your life and witness?

Don't diminish your vision to fit the realm of what currently seems possible. I wholeheartedly agree with the sentiments of author, Robert Fritz, who said, "If you limit your choices only to what seems possible or reasonable, you disconnect yourself from what you truly want, and all that is left is a compromise." Don't arrive at the end of your life only to discover how much more you could have become, done and had, if only you had envisioned more. Michelangelo said, "The greater danger for most of us is not that our aim is too high and we miss it, but that it is too low and we reach it."

Don't sabotage your vision by fixating on your past or present limitations. Remember that where you gaze is ultimately where you'll go. Too many of us "wreck" our lives because we are constantly focused on the things in life that we don't want, rather than steering toward the things that we desire. Everything begins with your vision. What do you see in your future? Don't worry about how it will come to pass, just get a clear life vision in your mind and spirit – one worth reviewing and meditating on daily – and watch the pieces begin to fall into place!

Keep God and His purposes at the center of your vision. You've been placed on earth to accomplish something great for Him. If your vision isn't God-centered, you'll run the risk of climbing the "ladder of success" only to find, after reaching the top, that it was leaned against the wrong "building" all along! Ultimately, as our Focus Verse teaches, the most important vision is not that which is visible, but that which is invisible. It is not that which is temporary, but that which is eternal.

Finally, with a clear, compelling vision anything is possible. Great visions attract great people, resources, and opportunities. Here's the amazing thing, it doesn't cost any more to dream big than it does to dream small! Have you started writing that vision yet?

TAKE ACTION!

Thoughts for your Journal:
Describe in realistic detail where you see yourself a year from now. What about 5 years from now?

Prayer Focus:
> ➤ Pray for insight to understand your purpose.
> ➤ Pray that God will grant you not just sight, but a clear vision of His   preferred future for your life.

Suggested Bible Reading:
> ➤ Proverbs 29
> ➤ Habakkuk 2: 1-4
> ➤ 2 Corinthians 4

Day Twenty-Seven
"It's Not You, It's Me!"

Focus Verse: *"Can two people walk together without agreeing on the direction?"* (Amos 3: 3 NLT)

One of the most used break-up lines of all time may well be, *"It's not you; it's me."* These words are aimed at putting a person out of one's life without putting them down. Usually they're anything but true. Sincerer words might be: "It's not me; it's ALL you." That you've traveled this far on this devotional journey indicates one thing: that you are serious about lasting life-change. So, today, I want to share another indispensable key to lasting personal growth. If you are serious about self-improvement, you must surround yourself with positive people who are going in the same direction as you are. Our Focus Verse poses the question, "Can two people walk together without agreeing on the direction?" Whether you realize it or not, everyone you allow into your close circle is someone with whom you have some level of agreement. Further, it is impossible to walk together unless you are going in the same direction! Therefore, in order to truly change our lives, we must begin today by taking a good, hard, honest look at those we are walking through life with. In what direction are they going? Are they moving closer to God? Are they moving closer to the life of our dreams? Or are they moving away from where we want to go?

It is not what you say, but who you are walking with that reveals who you really are – and also says a lot as to where you are going. At the risk of sounding corny, let me remind you that, "You can't fly with eagles if you are running with turkeys!"

Why do we hold onto people who are not headed where we wish to go? Well, there are several reasons. For one, often we still hang with them because they represent the familiar – we have known them a long time. We grew up around them, or they remind us of people from our familiar past. That is, we feel comfortable around them even though we feel that we have outgrown their ways.

Another reason we find it easy to be around people who don't share our aspirations for excellence is because they don't challenge us to be our best. They don't make us uncomfortable with failure or mediocrity.

Ultimately, and this is an uncomfortable truth, we hang with people who are not going the same direction we profess to be going, because beneath the surface, we are far more like them than we care to admit. Part of us wants to go in a positive direction – the other part of us doesn't want to exert the discipline and effort to change. So we are drawn to people who provide us with a ready-made excuse for our failure.

But, no more! That ends today. In order to arrive at Purpose, you must be willing to leave those you know are not going in the direction you aspire to. Simple – but not easy. Your destiny is at stake. Your ability to grasp everything God has promised you depends on mustering the courage and character to methodically remove those who will distract or detract from your walk of faith. David said, "...I will not know a wicked person.... he that telleth lies shall not tarry [stay] in my sight" (Psalm 101: 4b, 7b). Is it any wonder that he was called "a man after God's heart"? You cannot cling to worldly relationships and draw closer to God. Not possible. You cannot hold on to alliances that are moving away from your destiny and arrive where you are called to be. Are you really ready to become who you know you were created to be? Take inventory of the chambers of your heart, right now. Separate yourself from every relationship that is pulling you away from the direction of your promise!

For those people in your life who have no intention of changing or growing, I think that I may finally have found an appropriate and honest use for the tired old break-up line. You can let them down easy by truthfully saying, "It's not you; it's me." In other words, "It's not that you have done anything different, it's just that, well, I've changed. And the things that we used to have in common – like procrastination, failure and mediocrity – I've moved away from. In fact, I've moved on...to higher ground. I've changed my focus, my vision and my habits. It's not you; it's me!" Truthfully speaking, creating distance need not be dramatic. It can become a matter of simply not being as "available" as you once were.

However, it is not enough to distance yourself from wrong people in your life. You must also, starting today, make a conscious effort to gravitate toward and befriend those positive people who are going in the same direction as you are. Here are some questions that might help you to discern and recognize those individuals: Does being around this individual make me want to be closer to God? Does this relationship challenge me to be my best? Does this person share the same kinds of values, ethics and aspirations that I hold? Is this someone that I can share mutual encouragement and accountability with? Will this person demand excellence from me? These kinds of questions may move you out of your comfort zone, but that is a move in the direction of your destiny. In every arena of life – spiritual, professional, social, etc. – you must seek out the people who are going "your way" and gravitate toward them. Learn from them. If possible, forge alliances with them.

As you surround yourself with positive people progressing in the same direction, you will begin to experience accelerated personal growth, as you advance ever more rapidly up the road to your dreams. But it may well begin with the statement, "It's not you; it's me."

TAKE ACTION!

Thoughts for your Journal:
> ➢ When we have outgrown a garment, it no longer "fits" us comfortably. Can you think of any friendships that once "fit" well, but have now been outgrown in your life? In what ways do they no longer "fit"?
> ➢ List several positive relationships. In what ways do they enrich you or empower you to be better? Who among your acquaintances should you consider attempting to forge a closer relationship with?

Prayer Focus:
> ➢ Ask the Lord to both shrink and enlarge your circle. Ask Him to remove those in your inner circle who are hindering your progress, and to enlarge the circle of people who put forth a positive influence in your life.
> ➢ Pray for those in your life who encourage you, challenge you and empower you to be better! Ask God to bless and encourage them in the same way that they are an encouragement to others.

Suggested Bible Reading:
> ➢ Proverbs 13: 20
> ➢ Proverbs 22: 24-25
> ➢ I Corinthians 15: 33
> ➢ 2 Corinthians 6: 14-18

Day Twenty-Eight
True Worshippers

Focus Verses: *"But the hour cometh, and now is, when the true worshippers shall worship the Father in spirit and in truth: for the Father seeketh such to worship Him. God is a Spirit: and they that worship Him must worship in spirit and in truth."* (John 4: 23, 24 KJV)

Much of what we do in church is for the benefit of other people. We sing for others. Certainly, we preach for others. We pray in such a way that others will be impressed. Arguably, even some of our praise is tailored to impact others. No one ever said that what we offer to the Lord shouldn't also bless someone else, but I do want to point out that in trying to impress other churchgoers, there is a real and present danger of forgetting Who our true "audience" is. If I get too caught up in trying to impress people with my praise and worship, I run the risk of alienating God. As quiet as it is kept, God is not desperate for my worship – He actually has a full-time staff (24 hours a day; 7 days a week; 365 days a year) of angelic worshippers who do it better than me. He is in position to be selective as our Focus Verses show.

In the text from John's Gospel, Jesus encounters a Samaritan woman at a well. She is a scandalous, sinful woman, but she is also religious, and highly opinionated. Isn't that typical of human nature? Those who are least qualified to spout opinions are often the most vocal. On this particular day, she met her match. Jesus was on a mission of mercy and would not be deterred, not even by the woman's own self- imposed hindrances.

Briefly consider Jesus' words to her – "The hour cometh, and now is, when the true worshippers shall worship the Father in spirit and truth..." In other words, He tells her that her arguments about the place of worship are irrelevant, because true worship goes deeper than location. True worship must be in keeping with God's nature. God is a Spirit, and so real worship on His behalf must come from our spirit.

We are good at bringing worship from our flesh (that which is physically gratifying and pleasing to the eye), and from our soul (our will, mind and emotions), but what of our spirit? We don't even like to really address that part of our nature because the spirit is so unattended that we have difficulty even defining it. Yet our spirit is the part of our nature that was created to be most in alignment with God. The spirit is that part of us that actually hears God. It is that part of us that when understood, fed, and used properly gives us dominion in the earth. No matter how gratifying and exciting our worship is to the flesh and soul, it has little true relevance until it reaches down and awakens the deep things of our spirit, so that from our spirit we touch the deep things of God.

But worshipping from the spirit is not enough. He also said "in truth." Interestingly, in John's Gospel, truth is associated with Christ (14:6). So, for our worship to be "true," it must be spirit-based, but also Christ-centered. If others are blessed by what we bring to Christ, wonderful. But, that is not the primary consideration. We are called first and foremost to perform our acts of devotion for an audience of One, Jesus Christ. If at the end of the day, He is unimpressed with the authenticity of my praise and worship, I am a false worshipper – no matter how many people shouted, cried, "high-fived," or left inspired. He is the only observer of my worship who really matters. Yet how many times has pleasing Him with my worship been a secondary consideration? How many times have I ignored an impulse to lose myself in worship of Him because of some personal inhibition – not wanting to embarrass myself or seem out of control?

Lord, deliver us from the need to look to others like we have it all together. Our carefully crafted façades not only block others from seeing who we really are, they also keep us from seeing Your face, in all of Your beauty. Help us. So, change us that when You look at us, Your search for true worshippers can finally come to an end.

TAKE ACTION!

Thoughts for your Journal:
> ➤ What does it mean to worship the Lord in spirit and truth? How do you measure up?
> ➤ If the Father is seeking a certain kind of worshipper, what do you suppose the results might be when He finds what He is looking for?

Prayer Focus:
> ➤ Ask God to take away your inhibitions in praise and worship and to make your entire life a "song of praise" for His Glory!
> ➤ In your prayer time today, express your praise or worship to God in a way that you might not normally do – make up a song for Him, or perform a dance – do something to break out of the box of inhibition. Perform for an Audience of One!

Suggested Bible Reading:
> ➤ Proverbs 23
> ➤ Psalm 34

Fuel Stop
Change Your Settings!

Have you ever felt stuck? All of us at some time or other have felt stuck in an endless loop – thinking the same negative thoughts, clutching the same negative belief systems, speaking the same negative words, repeating the same self-defeating behaviors and experiencing the same disappointing results. Here's what the loop looks like: limiting thoughts create limiting mental images, which in turn limit our success, which reinforces the original limiting thoughts!

How do we end up feeling stuck? Because of thermostat settings – or to put it another way, comfort zones. Our comfort zone works the same way that the thermostat in our home works. Get this. When the temperature in the room reaches the edge of a temperature range that you have set, the thermostat sends an electrical signal to the furnace or the air conditioner to turn it on or off. As temperatures change, the thermostat setting continues to respond to those changes with electrical signals that keep the temperature within the desired range.

Did you get that? You and I have internal, psychological thermostats in our lives that regulate our level of performance.

Instead of electrical signals, our internal performance "thermostat" uses discomfort signals to keep us within our comfort zone. When our behavior or performance level arises to the edge of that zone, we begin to feel uncomfortable. When we begin to perform at a level – for better or worse – that is outside the self-image that we unconsciously hold, our internal "thermostat" will send signals of mental tension and physical discomfort to our system. To avoid the discomfort, we unconsciously pull ourselves back into our comfort zone.

Most of us have financial "temperature" settings. If our self-image is that we earn $40,000 a year, the tendency will be to produce that amount regardless of external circumstances, because to do anything else would make us uncomfortable. The positive side is that if times are hard, we will put in extra hours, work weekends, create new opportunities and do everything possible to reach that financial level. But the negative side is that if great opportunity arises, there will be the tendency still to do just enough to get that $40,000 we have become accustomed to earning.

But it doesn't stop there. As relates to your savings account you need to be aware that you have a thermostat there also. Some people are comfortable as long as they have $1,500 in savings. Others are uncomfortable with anything less than $25,000. Still others of us are comfortable with no savings at all and credit card debt of $15,000. Imagine for a moment that person whose comfort zone is $25,000 is hit with an unexpected medical expense of $10,000. What will she do? In all likelihood, she will curtail spending, work overtime, sell off possessions – do whatever is necessary to get that nest egg back up to $25,000.

Not to belabor the point, but most lottery winners end up broke again in just a few short years. Why? It is because their financial status changed, but not their mindset. Their internal psychological thermostat never changed and so it slowly brought them back to their original "comfort" zone of poverty.

We have psychological thermostats not only in the area of our finances, but in every area of our lives – relationships, tastes, spirituality, etc. Our greatest hindrance to living the lives we have dreamed about is not the devil, but our own devilish comfort zones. Let the following quote sink in:

"Everything you want is just outside your comfort zone."

Robert Allen

Breaking out of your comfort zone begins with seeing it for what it really is – a self- made prison. Originally built to protect you, it consists of the long list of cannots, musts, must nots, and other limiting beliefs accumulated over your lifetime.

Today, I want to challenge you to re-set your "thermostat." There are many ways to accomplish this, but perhaps the simplest and most effective way is through the power of Positive Affirmations. An affirmation is a statement that describes a goal in its already completed state, such as "I am feeling fit and fabulous at my ideal body weight of..."

You can shatter the limits of your current comfort zone and re-set your psychological thermostat by bombarding your subconscious mind with new thoughts and images of what you want your new comfort zone to look like – images of your goals completed and of your dreams fulfilled.

Simple Guidelines for Effective Affirmations

1. Start with the words I am. Starting your sentence with those words creates a command for your subconscious mind – something to make happen.

2. Use the present tense. Say it as though it is already happening for you.

3. Affirm what you want, not what you don't want.

4. Keep it brief. You want your affirmations to be memorable to you.

5. Be specific. Vague words produce vague results.

6. Make affirmations for yourself not for others. Your affirmations are to describe your own behavior, not that of others.

Create Your Affirmations List

Think about your various goals and...

➢ Visualize what you would like to make happen. See things as you would like them to be, as if you are inside the completed goal looking out on the world.

➢ Imagine the sounds and feelings that would accompany the completed goal.

➢ Describe what you are experiencing (the completed goal) in a brief statement that includes what you are feeling.

➢ If necessary edit your affirmation to be sure that it meets the guidelines outlined above.

Using Your Affirmations

1. Review your affirmations one to three times daily.
2. If you can, read each one aloud with passion. Visualize it as completed and imagine the sounds and feelings that might accompany the success described in the affirmation.
3. Say the affirmation again, and repeat this same process with the next affirmation.
4. Post your affirmations around your home on "3 x 5" cards.
5. Repeat your affirmations as often as you can throughout the day – in traffic, waiting in a line, working out, etc.
6. Record and listen to your affirmations.
7. Use them as your screensaver on your computer.

Words have power. God spoke and everything that we see came into being. You are in His image. You have the power to speak and see everything in your life change for the better. Why not begin to use that power? Change your settings!

Day Twenty-Nine
"Send Me...I'll GROW!"

Focus Verses: *""In the year that King Uzziah died, I saw the Lord sitting on a throne, high and lifted up, and the train of His robe filled the temple... So I said: "Woe is me, for I am undone! Because I am a man of unclean lips, And I dwell in the midst of a people of unclean lips; For my eyes have seen the King, The Lord of hosts."* (Isaiah 6: 1, 5 NIV)

As we end our Journey together, we will be spending these last three days with the Old Testament Prophet Isaiah. Those who are familiar with the 6th chapter of his prophecies, tend to think that Isaiah's acceptance of the Call of God was expressed in verse 8, when he said, "Here am I; send me." As I meditated on this passage, I saw something I had missed before: that Isaiah's surrender really was first expressed in the words of verse 5, *"Woe is me, for I am undone..."* Most Christians want to go for God, but few want to grow for Him. And yet fulfilling the call of God always requires growth, which makes most of us uncomfortable. Our problem with growth is this – it necessitates change. We tend to hate most change not initiated by us. We long to change the world without ourselves being changed. We want God to douse us with spiritual "Miracle-Gro" so that we can sprout up into greatness without going through any of the normal painful processes that accompany spiritual growth. Sorry to be the one to break this to you, but, it won't happen. In order to grow, you are going to have to do the fundamentals: start with the "sincere milk" of the Word; advance on to "spiritual meat;" submit to spiritual authority; accept reproof and correction; and prove yourself faithful in serving.

Your growth trajectory is determined by your willingness to change. No change tolerance, no growth. Little change tolerance, little growth. Great change tolerance, great growth. Remember, all change does not equal growth, but all growth equals change.

In what ways did Isaiah grow? There are several that come to mind:

He grew when he chose to humbly confess his own sins. Most of us have 20/20 vision when it comes to the sins of others, but are blind when it comes to seeing our own faults. Someone has observed that in the first five chapters of Isaiah's prophecies, his constant refrain is "Woe is..." Basically, "Woe is everyone!" But here in chapter six, after he has an encounter with the Glory of God, he is a changed man. He is able to see himself and be himself as he really is with no façade, no attempt to put on a front. That is what humility really means – the willingness to reveal the "real you."

After a while, the "perfection game" gets tiring – pretending that we are the perfect saint, the perfect mate, the perfect parent; that we have the ideal family, and the list could go on and on. I am not suggesting that we need to air all our dirty family laundry, only that we need an encounter with God that will cause us to take our masks off, and be real with ourselves and our God as to who we really are.

Isaiah grew when he acknowledged that there were things in his past and upbringing that had contributed to his spiritual delinquency. Isaiah said, "...and I dwell in the midst of a people of unclean lips." Sometimes, even harder than admitting that we have sinned and fallen short of the God's best, is admitting that the culture that we grew up with – whether our family, our community, our circle of friends, or even in some cases, our church – didn't really have it going on as much as we have led people to believe. That, again, requires humility – because, if we acknowledge that there are skeletons in our extended closet, then it may mean something is wrong with us. Could it be that some of the ways that we have done things for as long as we can remember weren't really the best or even the right way?

Isaiah grew when he acknowledged that he could see something better and purer than anything that he had ever experienced. "...for mine eyes have seen the King..." Isaiah was no stranger to royalty. He was cousin to the recently deceased King Uzziah, but the right vision and the right encounter gave him an entirely different understanding of what true Royalty is. Lord, open our eyes that we may see Your glorious wonders all around us. A person with a "been there, done that" mentality won't grow. He or she thinks they have already seen it all, or that they already know it all. Only someone who is open to seeing new things in God will continue to change and grow.

The question before us today is how ready are we to grow, really to grow? Are we willing to embrace and celebrate change in our lives as God works in us to will and to do of His good pleasure?

TAKE ACTION!

Thoughts for your Journal:
> ➤ What areas of change in your life has the Lord dealt with you on in this Journey?
> ➤ What disciplines and accountability are you going to set in place to help you to keep your commitment?

Prayer Focus:
> ➤ Ask the Holy Spirit to reveal the areas in which change is needed in your life, and give you the courage and strength to make those changes so that you can grow.
> ➤ Pray for wisdom to know the difference between needed change and unnecessary change.
> ➤ Pray for a spirit of repentance and spiritual growth to permeate the Church of Jesus Christ worldwide.

Suggested Bible Reading:
> ➤ Isaiah 6: 1-8
> ➤ Romans 12 & 13
> ➤ Hebrews 10 & 13

Day Thirty
"Send Me...I'll GIVE!"

Focus Verse: *"Also I heard the voice of the LORD, saying, 'Whom shall I send, and who will go for us?' Then said I, 'Here am I; send me.'"* (Isaiah 6: 8 KJV)

Today we revisit our discussion of Isaiah – the Old Testament prophet who not only volunteered to go and speak on God's behalf, but – who accepted the process of personal growth as preparation to go. Growing should almost always precede going. And as we learned yesterday, growth requires change and change is usually no fun. Whew! Glad we have completed that whole growth/change discussion. Are we packed and now ready to be sent? After all, as our Focus Verse tells us, God wants to know whom He can send. We're ready to answer the call, right? Well, taking a cue from Isaiah's response, it seems that we should say, "not so fast." There is yet another necessary prerequisite before we can be cleared for "takeoff." Before he went anywhere for God, Isaiah gave something.

You may be wondering, specifically how and what did Isaiah give? I submit to you that when he said, "Here am I..." Isaiah gave God the greatest gift that anyone can give – himself. Many Christians, even those who are generous in tithe and offerings, never get around to giving the greatest gift of all, themselves. In his letter to the church in the church in a city call Corinth, the Apostle Paul commends another congregation, the Macedonian church who gave lavishly to bless others in spite of their own abject poverty. The key to their being able to give beyond their own ability? They "...first gave their own selves to the Lord" (2 Corinthians 8: 5).

We modern Christians tend to use money either as a substitute or as an excuse. Those who have money and don't mind using it, often throw money out as a substitute for giving themselves. We send money where we ourselves don't want to go. Sometimes as parents we lavish our children with gifts in order to pacify them, when in reality they need us (our undivided, undistracted attention) far more than they need the latest expensive gadget or sneaker. We throw money at missions and giving to missions is extremely important – so that we can rest easy knowing that we never have to get our hands dirty by going on a missionary trip. What if God wants some of us, not just to send our money overseas, but to take it overseas? We throw money at the church projects so that we won't be expected to actually show up, roll our sleeves up and go to work. The point is that God doesn't just want your money, He wants all of you. He wants someone who will say "Here am I," not "I gave at the office."

We also use lack of money as an excuse for not doing the will of God. Many are quick to echo the words of Peter at the gate of the temple looking at the man in need of healing, "Silver and gold have I none..." (Acts 3: 6). But, of course, we never take it to the next level of saying, "...but, such as I have, give I unto thee." Instead, we rest on the lack of money as our alibi for never venturing forth into our divine destiny – for never making the difference we are called to make in the world. Lack of money, as an excuse, makes an appearance almost everywhere. We blame lack of money for not furthering our education. We blame it for not being a better spouse or parent. We blame it for not pursuing our ministry as we should – forgetting all the while, that we have within us a power greater than the power of silver or gold. If we can't give money, we can always give of ourselves. If we don't have money, that doesn't mean that we can't begin to walk toward our dreams. Money has a way of following vision. Vision never follows money.

Isaiah gave God himself. When we give ourselves, really give ourselves to God, He has our everything. There is nothing that I have that I will hide or withhold from Him when I have truly given myself. That is the most frightening of all commitments. It will cost me everything, even my life – but life from that moment will become a glorious adventure as I trust God in and for all things.

Let's eavesdrop on a conversation between Jesus Christ and one of his disciples, that rugged, brash fisherman, Simon Peter:

"Then Peter began to say to Him, 'Lo, we have left all and have followed Thee.'

And Jesus answered and said, Verily I say unto you, 'There is no man that hath left house, or brethren, or sisters, or father, or mother, or wife, or children, and lands, for My sake and the gospel's, But he shall receive an hundredfold now in this time houses and brethren, and sisters, and mothers, and children, and lands, with persecutions; and in the world to come eternal life.'"– Mark 10: 28-30 KJV

No matter how you wish to interpret this, it is an exciting and fulfilling promise! God will never let us be better to Him than He is to us! Yes, there will be persecution; there will be pain along the way, but there will also be unspeakable joy and indescribable blessing that goes along with the submitted life.

LORD, help us not only to be committed to grow and to give even before we attempt to commit to go.

TAKE ACTION!

Thoughts for your Journal:
- ➢ In what areas of your life have you either used money as a substitute or as an excuse in place of giving yourself?
- ➢ List ways in which you can be more giving?

Prayer Focus:
- ➢ Revisit your original "yes" to God. Recommit to giving yourself to Him above all else.
- ➢ Pray that the Lord will not only enable you to be more giving but that first He will make you more willing to give.

Suggested Bible Reading:
- ➢ Matthew 6
- ➢ 2 Corinthians 8 – 9
- ➢ Psalm 24

Day Thirty-One
"Send Me...I'll GO!"

Focus Verse: *"Also I heard the voice of the LORD, saying, 'Whom shall I send, and who will go for us?' Then said I, 'Here am I; send me.'"* (Isaiah 6: 8 KJV)

Over the past couple of days, we have discovered that only when we are fully committed to grow and fully committed to give ourselves completely, are we fully ready to move to the next step – ready to go for Him as ambassadors of God's Word and of His Love. Here we now stand, on the brink of destiny with the prophet Isaiah, as he answers the call of God, saying, "Here am I; send me." In a few short moments, in the glory of God, Isaiah has been transformed, fully committing himself to God. Now, he stands ready to be sent. Thinking about God's call to Isaiah, I noticed several peculiarities:

> ➢ God's call – "Whom shall I send, and who will go for us?" – offers no information as to where the Almighty intends to send His volunteer.

➢ God's call offers no insight regarding to whom He is sending His volunteer – will they be foreign or local? Hostile or friendly? Far or near?

➢ God's call gives no hint of a job description or title.

➢ God's call makes no reference to a compensation or retirement plan.

Who, in their right mind, would answer a call like this? A man who has grown in faith to the point of being able to say, "I trust God that He will do right by me, no matter what!" And one who has given himself totally over to the Master to the point of saying, "I am not my own; He can use me as He sees fit."

So easy to say. So hard to do. So necessary. I believe that each of us is called at some point in our lives to an encounter with destiny, perhaps a once in a lifetime encounter. We will be challenged by God – "Can I send you?" What will we say? Will we say, "Lord, can you give me a little more detail about this assignment; can I pray a while on it?" Or will we say, "Lord, I don't care where you send me – be it near or far. I don't care to whom you send me. I don't care what you ask me to do. I don't care about what comes with it – whether a title, personal glory or recognition. I say here and now, that as long as I know that it is You, my answer is, Yes, unconditionally!"

When we arrive at that point, we experience the truest meaning of abundant life. It seems as if scales fall off our eyes. The sun shines brighter; the world takes on a greater beauty and grandeur than we had ever before noticed. And we seem more alive to it. In fact, it seems as if, only then, are we truly alive. When we arrive at that point of full surrender, we are undergirded by a joy that makes the attendant trials and persecutions bearable.

I am reminded of the words of an old hymn we used to sing:

If Jesus Goes with Me

It may be in the valley, where countless dangers hide; It may be in the sunshine that I, in peace, abide; But this one thing I know – if it be dark or fair,

If Jesus is with me, I'll go anywhere!

Refrain:

If Jesus goes with me, I'll go anywhere!

'Tis heaven to me, where'er I may be, if He is there! I count it a privilege here, His cross to bear,

If Jesus goes with me, I'll go anywhere!

It is not mine to question the judgment of my Lord, It is but mine to follow the leadings of His Word; But if to go or stay, or whether here or there,

I'll be, with my Savior, content anywhere!

– Charles A. Miles (1908)

TAKE ACTION!

Thoughts for your Journal:

➢ Reflect on what it really means to be willing to "go" for the Lord. Are there areas in your life where you have put off obeying His call because of the need to grow more or to give Him more of yourself?

➢ As you near the end of this Journey, ask the Lord to show you any remaining areas of unforgiveness, bitterness, or other sins or hindrances that you have yet to fully place before Him.

Prayer Focus:

➢ Pray that as this Journey ends, you will never go back to "business as usual" in your walk with God.

➢ Pray that as you continually yield to the leading of the Holy Spirit, you will witness a mighty outpouring of the Power of God – in your life, your family, your church and your community!

Suggested Bible Reading:

➢ Ezekiel 22: 29-30
➢ Luke 5: 1-11
➢ Luke 9: 1-7, 57-62
➢ Acts 9

STAY CONNECTED

Thank you for purchasing, *Provisions for the Journey*. Bishop Moore would like to connect with you! Below are a few ways you can stay posted on new book releases, conferences, and speaking engagements.

INSTAGRAM @bishopmmoore
PERISCOPE BishopMMoore
FACEBOOK Mark Moore, Sr.
WEBSITE www.bishopmarkmoore.com

Made in the USA
Middletown, DE
26 June 2017